Where Rivers Flow

**Finding your way
   out of the desert
      with joy and gladness**

REBECCA MOORE

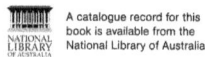
A catalogue record for this book is available from the National Library of Australia

Where Rivers Flow

Copyright 2023 ©Rebecca Moore

Published by Star Label Publishing
P.O. Box 1511, Buderim, QLD, Australia
publishing@starlabel.com.au

cover image: edited and created with licensed istock images

1st Edition May, 2023
All rights reserved. No part of this publication may be reproduced in any form; stored in a retrieval system; or transmitted; or used in any other form; or by any other means without prior written permission of the publisher (except for brief quotes for the purpose of review or promotion).

All Scripture quotations unless otherwise indicated are from The Holy Bible, New International Version®, NIV® Copyright © 1973, 1978, 1984, 2011 by Biblica, Inc.™ Used by permission. All rights reserved worldwide.

Scripture quotations marked (ESV) are from The Holy Bible, English Standard Version® (ESV®), copyright © 2001 by Crossway, a publishing ministry of Good News Publishers. Used by permission. All rights reserved.

The views expressed here-in remain the sole responsibility of the author, who exempts the publisher from all liability. The author and publisher do not assume responsibility for any loss, damage, or disruption caused by the contents, errors or omissions, whether such contents, errors, or omissions result from opinion, negligence, accident, or any other cause, and hereby disclaim any and all liability to any party.

ISBN: 978-0-6453697-6-2

To those who thirst...

'There is a river whose streams make glad the city of God, the holy place where the Most High dwells.'
Psalm 46:4

CONTENTS

FOREWORD	vii
ACKNOWLEDGEMENTS	ix
INTRODUCTION	xi
1. Where the River Flows, Everything Will Live	3
2. Don't Just Survive—Thrive!	9
3. Fruitful	15
4. Is the Grass Greener?	21
Poem—Contentment	27
5. A Good Coffee	31
6. Becoming Deliberate	37
7. Sonata No. 48 and the symphony of life	43
Poem—Resting Place	47
8. Finding Your Place To Flourish	49
9. Blurry Windows	55
10. The Great Jewel Heist	61
11. A Job Well Done	67
Poem—The Scribe	71
12. Small Beginnings are full of surprises	73
13. Don't Let Your God-fragrance End Up in the Belly of a Goat	79

14. Where There is Light, There is Hope	85
15. Stop Crying and Laugh	91
Poem—Her Home Beyond the River	97
16. Light Bulb Moments	99
17. Do You Hear the People Sing?	105
18. Up the Creek without a paddle	109
Poem – Be Still	113
19. When the cup is full	115
20. The Great Roar!	119
21. There's more to your pain than meets the eye	125
22. He will lift you up in due time	133
Poem – Oh let me dream!	141
23. Are you Really Listening?	143
24. Make a Joyful Noise	147
25. What makes God proud of us?	153
26. Is This A Dress Rehearsal?	157
Poem—I heard that You were coming	165
27. The Best Day Ever!	171
28. The Signet Ring	179
29. Weddings!	185
30. Though it has ended, yet, it has just begun	193
Poem – This New Day	199

FOREWORD

On reading Rebecca Moore's latest book *Where Rivers Flow* I was somewhat surprised by how practical and real her devotions are.

It is Practical

Rebecca deals with every day life in a clear and practical way. The reality of her humanity and dependence on God is refreshing in a performance driven world. Every life situation is linked to God's promises and His purpose for our lives.

It is Poetic

The use of language expressed through the gift of a poet was soul inspiring and uplifting, revealed within the rhythm and cadence of every new poem.

It is Prophetic

Woven through each story was a clear prophetic word from God's big picture for our lives. The sound of heaven can be heard clearly through each devotional chapter, bringing light, life and love from heaven above.

I found the book to be inspiring.

Pastor Steve Penny
Speaker, Author, Church Planter,
Leadership Consultant, 1000 SHIELDS

ACKNOWLEDGEMENTS

First and foremost, thank you Jesus – my best friend, the air I breathe, the One who gets me up in the morning with words of love and encouragement upon opening His wonderful Word. The One who shows me His love in the smallest of beautiful details in each day reminding me just how close He really is.
You will always have my heart,
You will always have my life.

To my husband Tony, whose river journey has been a winding one yet who has remained steadfast, strong and focussed, even in rocky terrain. Your love, endurance and trust in God, despite what comes our way, has inspired me to always push on, find ways to solve problems, and to rise to greater heights.

To my amazing children. Each of you are the pieces of my heart that I wear on the outside. So often my love overflows and rolls out my eyes. I am blessed and amazed by you every day.

To our children-in-love. God knew you'd be part of our family before you were born. You were always meant to be here, and we love you.

To our parents for their great love and support and for consistently *being there* for us. That kind of love cannot be measured, and we are so grateful.

Finally, in memory of my great writing mentor,

Dr Mark Tronson

who passed away July 2022. Thank you for believing in my writing and playing a big part in giving me the encouragement and confidence to try bigger and better things. You have given young writers around the world the opportunity to have their voices heard and have left a great legacy. I know you are enjoying your eternal reward in heaven.

My flesh and my heart may fail, but God is the strength of my heart and my portion forever.

Psalm 73:26

INTRODUCTION

When I began writing *Where Rivers Flow* (the third in my series of *Real World Devotionals that make you feel normal*) it was a very different world to the one we live in today. I didn't know what journey God was going to take me on, however, He gave the book title to my husband right at the beginning, and since then, everything has flowed into the shape of rivers. Just as rivers travel many different paths to get to their final destination, so too, does life for each one of us.

Having spoken in previous books of my own trials, blessings and even embarrassing moments, I have journeyed through years of rebuilding, trusting in God, and allowing Him to guide me even when things don't turn out the way I may have imagined. Though not always expected outcomes, God's ways are much more beautiful and purposeful than anything we can imagine or even plan for ourselves. They are complex, yet perfect. But first we must put our hand into His, even if blindfolded, and trust Him to guide us on the way that is right.

Coming out of a wilderness and walking into your destiny is exciting but still requires much faith. We will always need faith as we journey through our walk on this Earth. But just as a river travels over rocky ground, smooth ground, windy bends, and treacherous terrain, and even when that river feels dried up at times, we know that, with our eyes on Jesus, we will arrive at the crystal sea that stands before the throne of God.

The water of this river is life-giving, the trees that it waters flourish. My prayer is that whatever these past few years have poured upon you, that you will push forward with God, dance in the river, and be healed by the leaves on the trees growing either side.

Allow the river of God to wash away the old, refresh, cleanse and soothe the desert places within you, replenish the thirsty, bring new growth, healing, abundance and provision, grow new fruit, and give you peace. And may rivers of living water flow from within you (John 7:38) and as it flows from the Source of Life, may it pour out for the healing of the nations. Now, let's sail down the river together ...

> Then the angel showed me the river of the water of life, as clear as crystal, flowing from the throne of God and of the Lamb down the middle of the great street of the city. On each side of the river stood the tree of life, bearing twelve crops of fruit, yielding its fruit every month. And the leaves of the tree are for the healing of the nations.
>
> (Revelation chapter 22 verses 1-2)

And when it seems there's nothing left
Just look and you will find
That 'nothing' is for something new
which 'nothing' will remind.

For when you lose the days you knew
Which now are left behind
The day that's here will ask of you
For something new to find.

Rebecca Moore

Chapter 1

WHERE THE RIVER FLOWS, EVERYTHING WILL LIVE

My arms were getting tired, and I could feel the skin wearing from my elbows with all the backward paddling I was doing. Yet, there was something so refreshing and exhilarating about sitting in a tube on a river of fresh mountain water, and I was only too keen to get back in the flow.

Only seconds before, I had felt the thrill of being taken effortlessly down the small rapids, but now I had somehow come out of the flow, my floatable tube thrown to the side of the river with me on it, and I seemed to be going nowhere.

As I battled to get back to the middle where the river flowed best, sometimes it took a nudge from the tour guide's boat, but more often it took persistent paddling from me, often requiring me to get out of the tube to redirect it away from the snags and point it in a new direction.

Seasons of struggle
There have been many seasons in my life where I knew I was on the right river, but the struggle was fierce and the battle, wearing. My body, mind and spirit were being tested, and my muscles were building – though sore.

There are also times when God calls us to relax in Him, to let Him take the reins, where we are to pull in our arms and legs and let His current take us to where He wants us to go. These times require trust; a strong leaning into God. They can be fast paced, yet once you let go and let God, they are effortless.

When I found myself back in the centre of the flow of the river, I could relax; the strength of the current directing me in the strongest flow and eventually to the shore.

The river from the temple
One of my favourite verses in the Bible is Psalm

chapter 46 verse 4 that speaks of the river flowing from the temple where God dwells:

> There is a river whose streams make glad the city of God, the holy place where the Most High dwells.

I love this verse because it speaks to me of refreshment in God's great power, yet the gentleness of it being as flowing water coming straight from the source of all creation. It holds so much hope, promise, truth and healing, and I want anything that comes straight from Him.

This river is spoken of in more detail in Ezekiel chapter 47:

> The man brought me back to the entrance to the temple, and I saw water coming out from under the threshold of the temple toward the east (for the temple faced east.)
>
> …As the man went eastward with a measuring line in his hand, he measured off a thousand cubits and then led me through water that was ankle-deep. He measured off another thousand cubits and led me through

> water that was knee-deep. He measured off another thousand and led me through water that was up to the waist. He measured off another thousand, but now it was a river that I could not cross, because the water had risen and was deep enough to swim in—a river that no one could cross. (verses 1, 3-5)

We see here that as the river of God flows, it does not dry up – it gets deeper!

Verse eight shows us the life source coming out of this river:

> He said to me, "This water flows toward the eastern region and goes down into the Arabah, where it enters the Dead Sea. When it empties into the sea, the salty water there becomes fresh. Swarms of living creatures will live wherever the river flows. There will be large numbers of fish, because this water flows there and makes the salt water fresh; so where the river flows everything will live."

The river of God is also a provider of good things:

> Fishermen will stand along the shore; from En Gedi to En Eglaim there will be places for spreading nets. The fish will be of many kinds—like the fish of the Mediterranean Sea. But the swamps and marshes will not become fresh; they will be left for salt. (verses 10-11)

The river flowing from the temple brings much fruit and healing to the nations:

> Fruit trees of all kinds will grow on both banks of the river. Their leaves will not wither, nor will their fruit fail. Every month they will bear fruit, because the water from the sanctuary flows to them. Their fruit will serve for food and their leaves for healing. (verse 12)

Water quenches thirst, heals wounds, soothes dryness, hydrates desert places. A river nourishes anything it flows past, gives life to creation below the water and above, and feeds the land, giving shade, nourishment and life-giving food.

It is only fitting that God would use a river to describe His great flow of love to us, one that fulfils our every need and nourishes us on so many levels. I don't know about you, but I want to immerse myself in it, soak in it and drench myself with it. I want to be surrounded by it, find comfort by it and let my soul be refreshed by it.

This river can be found through Jesus.

> Come to me, all you who are weary and burdened, and I will give you rest. Take my yoke upon you and learn from me, for I am gentle and humble in heart, and you will find rest for your souls. For my yoke is easy and my burden is light.
> (Matthew chapter 11 verses 28-30)

Chapter 2

DON'T JUST SURVIVE—THRIVE!

Today, two things stood out to me. Firstly, as I drove into my driveway, two butterflies circling each other flew in front of my car. My mind was thrown back in time to when the world changed in 2020 with our first lockdown. It was a time of uncertainty for all, and we didn't really understand what was happening, but at the same time, our town was taken over by migrating butterflies. These were a beautiful reminder that, while the caterpillar is enclosed within the chrysalis, it is becoming something new, and when released, creates a beautiful landscape of colour as we saw when a kaleidoscope of butterflies coloured our vision.

Secondly, I watched as an eagle began to ascend into the skies just in front of our home above the valley. I watched as the smaller birds tried to peck at it and pull it down at a certain height, and I watched as the eagle surpassed their reach and soared higher and higher with barely a movement of its wings until it flew into the sun where I could no longer see it.

Both the butterflies and the eagle had major obstacles to overcome. For the butterfly, the chrysalis represents a dark place, isolated and alone. But during the dark days of the chrysalis, greater things are happening, and the glory of the butterfly is eventually released in all its beauty.

For the eagle to overcome its adversaries, it had to rise above them, and when the eagle reached the great heights, the air space where it had been attacked was so far away, it was just a distant memory.

God's kindness
I've recently been reading about Joseph in Genesis chapter 39. You probably know the story, but at this stage, he had been sold by his brothers and was now living in the household of an Egyptian named Potiphar. Joseph had been through some very dark days and his brothers led his own father to believe that he was dead. But God had not abandoned Joseph quite the opposite.

The Lord was with him so much that it was apparent to Potiphar that the favour of the Lord was upon Joseph. God made Joseph successful in everything he did and he was eventually put in charge of Potiphar's whole household. Verse four tells us that Potiphar entrusted to Joseph's care everything he owned.

> From the time he put him in charge of his household and of all that he owned, the LORD blessed the household of the Egyptian because of Joseph. The blessing of the LORD was on everything Potiphar had, both in the house and in the field.
>
> (Genesis chapter 39 verse 5)

Enter more obstacles

Just when things were settling down for Joseph, along comes Potiphar's wife who falsely accuses Joseph, landing him in prison. But God did not abandon him in prison either. Verses 20-21 tell us:

> But while Joseph was there in the prison, the LORD was with him; he showed him kindness and granted him favour in the eyes of the prison warden.

Once again, Joseph was held in such high esteem that the prison warden put Joseph (a prisoner) in charge of all those held in the prison, and he was made responsible for all that was done there (verse 22).

> The warden paid no attention to anything under Joseph's care, because the LORD was with Joseph and gave him success in whatever he did.
> (Genesis chapter 39 verse 23)

Thriving in the midst of obstacles
It didn't matter where Joseph was or what circumstances he was in – whether exalted in the palace or in the depths of a prison – God NEVER abandoned him. Joseph didn't just survive – he thrived!

He was given as much favour in the prison as he was in the household. Eventually, he would wear the signet ring of Pharoah and be trusted with the whole land of Egypt. Joseph's relationship with God and his obedience to Him would later save the people from starvation during the seven-year famine.

Hope for the future
There are many who feel locked up in this time; there are many who are physically locked up in this time.

It may seem like the way out of these dark days is far beyond the reach of what can be conceived. I'm sure Joseph felt like this many times, however, while in the dark places, God was creating something beautiful, just like the butterflies, and the impact would be powerful.

With our eyes on Jesus, we will one day see Him in the clouds when He comes to gather us. And as we reign for a thousand years in the land that God is giving us (Revelation chapter 20 verses 1-5), the dark days will be a very distant memory as with the eagle, in fact, they will be remembered no more.

In the meantime, seek His face, read His words, soak it in and find out what God wants you to do here and now to bring hope to a hurting world.

For this is the hope to come:

> But be glad and rejoice forever in what I will create,
> For I will create Jerusalem to be a delight and its people a joy.
> I will rejoice over Jerusalem
> And take delight in my people;
> The sound of weeping and of crying will be heard in it no more.

Never again will there be in it an infant who lives but a few days,
or an old man who does not live out his years;
the one who dies at a hundred will be thought a mere child;
the one who fails to reach a hundred will be considered accursed.

They will build houses and dwell in them;
they will plant vineyards and eat their fruit.
No longer will they build houses and others live in them, or plant and others eat.

For as the days of a tree, so will be the days of my people;
my chosen ones will long enjoy the work of their hands.

They will not labour in vain, nor will they bear children doomed to misfortune;
for they will be a people blessed by the LORD, they and their descendants with them.

(Isaiah chapter 65 verses 18-23)

Chapter 3

FRUITFUL

One of the downsides of living on rural land is our reliance on tank water. When we run out, we run out, and unless we've had rain to fill our reserve tank, we need water deliveries to get us by until the weather is favourable again.

Following a dry winter and multiple water deliveries, we arrived home from a function recently only to turn on our taps to find, once again, no running water. Thankfully we had a small amount in our reserve tank from a recent rain shower, and our water delivery would only be a 48 hour wait. (This can feel like a long time with not much water and a house full of people!)

Within a few hours after the water had been delivered, the clouds opened up, and we had the best rainfall we've had in months, filling our tank from partly full to mostly full – double the blessing!

Thanks to the blessing of rain, our sheep are now enjoying greener pastures, and everything has flourished and been refreshed!

Refreshment

Often in life, we can go through times of dryness and barrenness. During those times, it's difficult to see that there will ever be a 'break in the weather'. We watch as the green grass turns brown, the flowers fade away, and the colours seem to disappear. But one thing we can be assured of is that, just like the changing of weather with each season, so too the circumstances in our lives are sure to change.

I remember going through a very difficult time years ago that seemed to continue forever. I remember thinking that one day I would want to return to my past self and tell myself all the promises that were to be fulfilled. Casting my mind forward like that helped me see beyond the wilderness I was in and gave me hope.

Sure enough, God was faithful, and I am seeing His promises in my life being fulfilled. I also know that the wilderness was a training ground, growing my muscles of endurance to be able to withstand the challenges that we face today.

Unlikely places

In ways that only God knows how, He will take our weaknesses, prune us, grow us, and create stronger branches that bear fruit and create shelter for others. God will always make a way through our wilderness and sometimes it may come from the most unlikely places.

In Ezekiel chapter 17, God gives a word and says,

> I myself will take a shoot from the very top of a cedar and plant it; I will break off a tender sprig from its topmost shoots and plant it on a high and lofty mountain. (v. 22)

The topmost shoots of a tree are generally very small and twiglike. They are held up by the tree and its branches, and though unlikely to be thought of as strong, they take the brunt of the weather, building up resilience to survive the harsh conditions.

> On the mountain heights of Israel I will plant it; it will produce branches and bear fruit and become a splendid cedar. Birds of every kind will nest in it; they will find shelter in the shade of its branches. (v. 23)

In this replanting, the small shoot is given new life and grows strong branches to bear fruit and to give refreshment to others. The so-called drought in the lives of many who are feeling stagnant, is not for nothing, 'for you know that your labour in the Lord is not in vain.'(1 Corinthians chapter 15 verse 58)

It is, however, the training ground, the growing place, the strong foundation where fruit will be grown that will be sweet to the taste and used to edify and strengthen those around you. You will be able to withstand the storms because your roots will spread deep into the nourishing soil you have been planted in, creating sturdiness.

When you least expect it
So, when you think the land is barren and there is no hope, know that there is a rain cloud coming to pour water upon the earth, nourishing it, soaking it, and restoring life back into it. Green shoots will begin to sprout through the once dry ground, and trees and flowers will begin to grow. Livestock will find new strength and the trees of the field will seem to be clapping their hands.

> Now he who supplies seed to the sower and bread for food will also supply and increase your store of seed and will enlarge the harvest of your righteousness. You will be enriched in every way so that you can be generous on every occasion, and through us your generosity will result in thanksgiving to God.
>
> (2 Corinthians chapter 9 verses 10-11)

Despite what we see happening in the world, there is new birth, new hope, a breath of God upon the earth, a breath that wakes up its sleepers, that opens the eyes of the blind, that opens deaf ears giving hope and life to those who have been in the wilderness. Those who are wise are awake to it. Those who receive it, are revived by it.

> Wake up, sleeper, rise from the dead, and Christ will shine on you.
>
> (Ephesians chapter 5 verse 14)

Chapter 4

IS THE GRASS GREENER?

I often find myself writing about our pet goat. It's not that I'm particularly fond of him – the Lord knows how many times I've had to chase that goat away from my roses and the neighbour's garden when he escapes! He can be very infuriating, and threats of goat curry often enter my conversations at these times (though I never would).

The challenge
Our goat has, however, exhibited an intriguing habit since being a kid. Although a large part of our property is fenced off for the sheep and goat to roam and graze, our goat spends a great part of his days with his head poking through the wire fence trying to eat the grass on the other side. We have an even track on the other side

of our fence that he has managed to keep low at much effort and discomfort to himself.

Feeling sorry for him, my husband will often take the goat to the other side of the fence and tether him so he can eat as much of that grass as he likes. Yet, when given the opportunity to have his fill, we're always amazed that when this happens, the goat will sit and not eat anything! It must be that it's now too easy.

The escape artist
Our goat also likes to wander. My husband has spent much time positioning and mending our fences to restrict the goat from going where he shouldn't. We have been enjoying a time of great satisfaction with no real escapes having happened for a few months. Success!

Or so we thought, until a few days ago we woke to the sound of our bleating goat coming from the neighbour's yard. On further investigation we discovered that the goat had had a sleep over on their property and was now ready and wanting to come home. Go figure!

So, to summarise – the goat likes to eat the grass that is hard to get to, until it is no longer hard to get to, and when he escapes, he eventually realises that what he originally had was better, and now wants to return home. On return to his pasture, he proceeds to stick his head through the fence again and resume old habits. Hmmmm …

Proverbs has a lot to say about this kind of behaviour (read chapter 26), and Jesus depicts the difference between sheep and goats in Matthew chapter 25 verses 31-46. I could pretty much leave this story right here and you, the reader, would understand and have enough to think about. But let's delve a little deeper …

Finding contentment in an unsettled world
We often hear the phrase "the grass is greener on the other side", and yet, just as our goat discovered – it's not – and once on the other side, well…it's just boring.

It seems our society, just like the goat, lives largely in a state of discontent. While satisfaction and contentment are constantly being sought through many different means such as finance, relationships, job promotions, travel, retail therapy, drugs, alcohol etc. it is ultimately a short-lived, unsatisfying journey. We are seeing increasing rates of mental and health problems as a result of people not finding contentment.

A change of perspective may be in order. If your house is too small, perhaps it's because the house you have is bursting with blessings. If your relationships are suffering, perhaps there's a lot of potential improvement waiting to be found by investing in those who are suffering. If your job is not satisfying, perhaps there are opportunities to look for to expand and improve, or maybe pray for wisdom and open doors in finding a job more suited.

In the meantime, is there someone at your work who needs your friendship, counsel or kindness? Is there someone in your home that needs your focus and understanding, forgiveness and love? Is there undiscovered beauty in the circumstances you find yourself at present?

Where permanent contentment is found
Whilst in prison, Paul writes of the contentment he had found. This contentment was not dependent on circumstances, nor was it suddenly given to him at birth. It was a contentment he had discovered throughout years of living, in finding the true source of where his peace lies. It was not found in the place he dwelt, for prison is not luxurious by any means; it was not found in youth or beauty, for he was aged and

lacking basic needs; it was not found in work, or things, or people. It was found in God.

> …for I have learned to be content whatever the circumstances. I know what it is to be in need, and I know what it is to have plenty. I have learned the secret of being content in any and every situation, whether well fed or hungry, whether living in plenty or in want. I can do all this through him who gives me strength.
> (Philippians chapter 4 verses 11-13)

We can learn a lot from nature. God was not accidental in how He made His creation. Perhaps we can learn more from the sheep who stay within the pasture that is already flowing with green grass and blessings. May the Lord give us eyes to see what we have already been given, and may He bless it and give us wisdom in how to best use it for His glory.

> But godliness with contentment is great gain. For we brought nothing into the world, and we can take nothing out of it. But if we have food and clothing, we will be content with that. Those who want to get rich fall into temptation and a trap and

into many foolish and harmful desires that plunge people into ruin and destruction. For the love of money is a root of all kinds of evil. Some people, eager for money, have wandered from the faith and pierced themselves with many griefs.

    (1 Timothy chapter 6 verses 6-12)

POEM

CONTENTMENT

I may not know the sum of all
The things this world withholds,
But there are things that I hold dear
Within this world I know:

I know just what it's like to hold
my babies in my arms,
To see their little eyes on mine,
So lost within their charms.

I know just what it's like to feel
the heartache and the loss,
And treasure each last moment
Of a friend to illness lost.

I know just what it's like to know
the love of one so dear,
Where life and love and reason
Dispels all other fear.

I know just what it's like to miss
the years that go before,
And realise just how precious
Are those moments, now no more.

I know just what it's like to know
that dreams lie up ahead,
There's always hope, there's always love,
There's more path yet to tread.

And I can yet imagine
all the things I do not know,
For empathy, compassion,
are the boat in which I'll row.

And pain and love go hand in hand
with everything that's been,
The one thing that we share the most,
is that which is unseen.

So we fix our eyes not on what is seen, but on what is unseen, since what is seen is temporary, but what is unseen is eternal.
(2 Corinthians chapter 4 verse 18)

Chapter 5

A GOOD COFFEE

A good coffee is worth waiting for. A few decades ago, instant coffee was a big seller. It was quick and versatile; you could keep it in the cupboard for a few months and even pack it in your picnic bag.

As Australians became acquainted with the introduction of percolated coffee and its flavour varieties, we began to acquire a more sophisticated taste. This ultimately shifted to espresso coffee as we know it today, with beans picked from carefully selected coffee vegetations around the world – each with distinct flavours, farm histories and worker standards being taken into consideration. Following this, the beans go through selective processes of roasting, grinding, brewing, extraction, separation, and presentation.

Each of these processes have processes of their own, resulting in a final onslaught of options for the coffee connoisseur, ranging from: espressos, café lattes, macchiatos, affogatos, flat whites, my husband's favourite – triple ristretto lattes, and the list goes on.

Australians now boast some of the best coffee in the world and many of us have become, what is termed, coffee-snobs.

Totally worth it!
The years and processes involved in bringing us these finely crafted drinks is well appreciated, so much so that it is difficult to go back to how we once drank coffee, even though at the time it was the best we knew.

Endurance is the key
Sometimes in life we feel like we are going through long drawn out processes, a bit like the journey of the coffee bean. Sometimes we feel picked or chosen, we may go through times of roasting or being judged by others, some grinding may be involved where we feel trials weighing us down, and brewing can sometimes last for years before the extraction of our gifts are identified and brought out.

There can be separation involved in following the path our newly discovered gifts are taking us on and of letting go of past careers/locations if that is required to accommodate for the new. Finally, there is the presentation where our process has come full circle and we have been finely crafted and moulded into what God had originally ordained for us to consistently walk in as revelation follows.

There is no real short-cut. The process is important in extracting the full aromatic flavours that God the Creator has predestined for us. The journey requires endurance, patience, faith and commitment on our part, and words like patience and endurance are not necessarily things we want to put our hand up for.

Knowing who to follow
Just like when the Israelites left Egypt and began their journey to the Promised Land, we have to know whom we are following. For the Israelites, God appeared to them as a pillar of cloud by day and a pillar of fire by night.

He led them, not by the short 11-day route, but on a path that would take them 40years to complete before entering their promised land. There was a lot to be learnt on this journey and God knew that if they took the short route, they would turn back to their oppression at the first sign of trouble.

> When Pharaoh let the people go, God did not lead them by way of the land of the Philistines, although that was near. For God said, "Lest the people change their minds when they see war and return to Egypt." But God led the people around by the way of the wilderness toward the Red Sea.
> (Exodus chapter 13 verses 17-18 ESV)

It was only as they learnt to trust God to be their deliverer, provider, protector and guide, did they gain traction towards the arrival to the Promised Land. Still, there were many who fell by the wayside, lacking faith and obedience, who never entered into the promise.

For those who received their reward, there was great celebration, and altars were set in place so that the journey would never be forgotten by the generations to come.

A full-bodied bean
It is no short-term trip or journey that we're on. Relationship with God needs to be developed, and for

those who persevere, persist, and endure, while also enjoying the provision, protection, and love of God – the Promised Land awaits.

As we are developed into full-bodied beans with a pleasant aroma that wafts beyond ourselves and onto those around us, let us keep our eyes on the One who goes before us and know that He is always present, and nothing goes to waste.

> For God is not unjust so as to overlook your work and the love that you have shown for his name in serving the saints, as you still do. And we desire each one of you to show the same earnestness to have the full assurance of hope until the end, so that you may not be sluggish, but imitators of those who through faith and patience inherit the promises.
> (Hebrews chapter 6 verses 10-12 ESV)

Chapter 6

BECOMING DELIBERATE

Who knows how quickly a week can pass and you haven't stopped for a breath? "Oh look, it's Thursday already!" I often hear myself say, and it only feels like a couple of days since I said it a week earlier. If we're not careful, weeks turn into months and years, and we hardly notice.

Being deliberate

When my teenagers return to school following holidays, I miss them. I miss having them around, going on bushwalks and picnics together and planning family activities that we don't make the deliberate effort to do quite so often during the school term.

I find that during the first couple of weeks into the school term, I am deliberate in my interactions with my children outside of school/work hours; I will spend deliberate time chatting with them after school, I will spend deliberate time saying goodnight to them at bedtime, and I will spend deliberate time being interested in organising purposeful weekend activities.

Fast forward three or four weeks and I find myself back in the rat-race of regular activities, the motion of repetition, the familiar and thoughtless rut of routine, and before I know it, I have to snap myself out of it and remind myself to be deliberate again. Anyone relate?

Work it into your day
To help combat this run-ragged routine, my eldest daughter and I realised we needed to exercise to keep our minds and bodies fresh and alert. We knew the only way we could commit ourselves to exercising regularly, was to work it into our day. It would need to be somewhere easily accessible, at the same time, and not overwhelming so as to put us off or seem too difficult. We would need to be deliberate.

By exercising together, we kept each other on task, and before we knew it, we had kept this daily event for four consecutive months! We have now developed a habit, and what felt like something we had just begun, we now realise those days turned into weeks which turned into months and will hopefully turn into years.

How deliberate are we when it comes to God?
Though I find myself chatting with God often throughout the day, being deliberate in prayer time can sometimes be an area vulnerable to distraction.

I was recently reading in Exodus about the Tent of Meeting. This is where Moses would meet to enquire of the Lord. This was a very deliberate place for Moses to meet with God, so much so, that whenever Moses entered the tent:

> ...a pillar of cloud would come down and stay at the entrance while the Lord spoke with Moses. Whenever the people saw the pillar of cloud standing at the entrance to the tent, they all stood and worshiped, each at the entrance of their tent. The Lord would speak to Moses face to face, as one speaks to a friend.
> (Exodus chapter 33 verses 10-11)

Moses would talk with God and God would answer him. They would have conversations *'face to face, as one speaks to a friend'*. How awesome is that!

Sometimes we forget that because of Jesus' sacrifice to banish the divide between God and His children, we have the same access where we can speak to God as a friend – the holiest of holy friends.

What does your Tent of Meeting look like?
Thinking on these things, I have begun writing a prayer journal again. For me, this has become my Tent of Meeting. This is where I write to God and He answers me, sometimes while I am still writing, other times a bit later. We have conversations which go beyond the paper, but the act of writing causes me to be deliberate in my thoughts and words. Because I like writing, this works well for me and I can return to previous prayers and see how they have been answered.

What does your Tent of Meeting look like, or what could it look like? You may prefer to incorporate your prayer in a deliberate daily prayer walk as a few of my close friends like to do. It may look different again to that, but whatever your chosen Tent of Meeting looks like, make it deliberate, make it regular and meet *'face *to face, as one speaks to a friend'* with the Creator God who longs to talk with you and be involved with your daily life.

At first it may need scheduling to help make it a routine, but whether you put it in your diary or on an alarm on your phone, turn it into a habit and before you know it, those days will have become weeks, months and years and you will have amazing answered prayers to celebrate all the way through; prayers that will change the course of your future and the future of others.

> Therefore I tell you, whatever you ask for in prayer, believe that you have received it, and it will be yours.
> (Mark chapter 11 verse 24)

Chapter 7

SONATA NO. 48 AND THE SYMPHONY OF LIFE

Sometimes I can be a bit of a music nerd. I love classical music and often get wrapped up in songs, so I'd like to give a disclaimer right up front, that throughout this story, I may get carried away with some obvious clichés and analogies.

Joseph Haydn's Sonata No. 48 is one of my favourite pieces to play on the piano. It is a complicated piece, which is partly why I love it, but I rather enjoy how the movements throughout the 12 pages take me on a journey through a story filled with crescendos and decrescendos until ending a satisfying completion at the composer's designated destination. It connects with my soul causing me to reflect on life and pour my emotions through the music.

It's a song I have been playing for many years now and I know it very well but, put someone in the room while I'm playing it, and all of a sudden I have to start reading the music. I make slips I wouldn't normally make, and I find I have to concentrate just a little bit more to bring out the easy flow I would normally play when it has my complete focus.

Distractions

When I have an audience, if I don't focus on the song, I get distracted. It's not that anyone is being noisy; I get distracted because my mind wanders from the music to the person in the room. *Have I played too long? Are they're bored? What do they think of this piece? Perhaps they're not comfortable and might need a seat?* Whatever the thoughts, at this point I'm not concentrating enough on the music that's been given to me to make the song sound as beautiful as it should.

When God created us, He knew us before we were born. He gave us gifts and purpose, and promised to bring to completion the good work that He had begun in us (Philippians chapter 1 verse 6). But sometimes in the desire to please others, or just in the process of living life, we get distracted and turn our focus onto 'the man' instead of keeping our focus on the Creator and His Word.

Keeping the song in key

The enemy knows that when we are in tune with God, seeking His way and purpose for our lives, we are capable of doing incredible things for the Kingdom. We become dangerous. When our eyes are fixed on God, our lives play through a beautiful melody with many colourful movements. Sometimes life is lived at *Andante* – a walking pace, and other times it is *Allegro* – fast, quick and bright. Finally, we are lifted to the triumphant heights of a victorious ending and the song is brought to a beautiful completion.

But if we get distracted, the song begins to sound distorted. It can take some turns that really hurt our ears, and until it gets back in the correct key that it was meant to be played in, it's really hard to listen to.

God, the great composer

God is the greatest composer of the music of our lives. He has written the perfect music for us to learn from – the Bible; given us the perfect example to shape our lives from – Jesus; and has given us the greatest conductor to help us navigate our way through each and every note – The Holy Spirit. If we trust in Him to conduct us through all the movements, the finished composition will be stirring, life-changing, beautiful to listen to, and uniquely written for each person.

And even if we have begun a little shaky, Jesus makes everything beautiful in His timing.

> He put a new song in my mouth, a hymn of praise to our God. Many will see and fear the Lord and put their trust in him.
> (Psalm chapter 40 verse 3)

POEM

RESTING PLACE

I dare not leave this resting place,
a place where I can rest.
If time or space did find an end,
this still would be my nest.
He covers me in feathers
and underneath His wings,
I curl up in this treasure
and to His arms I cling.

And in this place I stay,
a constant source of peace,
While still, my soul is resting calm,
my body doesn't cease.
While busy in life's busyness
and all the goings-on,
There is a place, there is a space,
where quietness is strong.

Rebecca Moore

He sees my coming and my going,
He sees my ardent needs.
He feels my love, He feels my pain,
He sees all that I see.
To be in places both at once,
an earthly skill unknown,
But what I know is possible
– with Him, it is my home.

For deep within,
my resting soul is closely knit to Him.
While busy is the earthly cloak
He gave me made of skin,
My resting place is wrapped and swaddled,
right beside His chest.
It's where I hear his heartbeat,
it's where I find my rest.

He will cover you with his feathers, and under
his wings you will find refuge.
(Psalm 91:4)

Chapter 8

FINDING YOUR PLACE TO FLOURISH

Times have certainly changed rapidly in the past few years. I don't think anyone has been untouched by this new way of life. It's almost as if the turn of 2020 also turned on a switch that changed normal into unnormal. Such times have required much from us: to stretch, grow, test, and think differently. But, though circumstances change, God never changes and neither does His love for us.

In Genesis chapter 26, we read about Isaac, the son of Abraham through whom descendants, as numerous as the stars in the sky, would be birthed. During a famine in the land, Isaac went to live in the land of the Philistines in Gerar. This land of his enemies would one day belong to his own descendants just as God had promised.

God's promises never fail but may take a journey

While Isaac lived in this land, he planted crops which reaped a hundredfold within the same year, because the Lord blessed him (v.12). He became very rich and because the Philistines envied him, they attacked him by filling up the wells that had been dug during the time of Abraham. King Abimelek, therefore, told Isaac to move away as he had become too powerful for them.

I imagine this would have been unsettling for Isaac seeing as he had established his fields and was accumulating great wealth. He would now have to uproot and leave the place where he had been blessed so much from the Lord. However, wherever Isaac went, the God he served was with him.

During the process of moving away, Isaac found a well that had belonged to his father Abraham but had been filled with earth by the Philistines. When his servants dug and found fresh water, the herders of Gerar quarrelled saying the water was theirs. So, Isaac moved on and dug another well. Once again, they quarrelled with him that the water was theirs, until he moved on yet again and dug another well. This one no one quarrelled over.

> Now the Lord has given us room and we will flourish in the land.
>
> (Genesis chapter 26 verse 22)

Finding the place where you will flourish

God had to move Isaac until he was at the place where He would flourish him. God knew where it was, but Isaac had to go through a series of obstacles until he found it.

Isaac must have been feeling the weight of the upheaval in a land of people rejecting him and moving him on, threatening his peace and place of existence. Thankfully God knows all our thoughts and feelings and meets us where we are:

> That night the Lord appeared to him and said, "I am the God of your father Abraham. Do not be afraid, for I am with you; I will bless you and will increase the number of your descendants for the sake of my servant Abraham."
>
> (Genesis chapter 26 verse 24)

And God did establish him and give him peace. God put His seal upon him that was obvious to those around him. Those who had sent him away, including the king, came and found him and met with him and made a treaty with him, because they saw that the blessing of the Lord was on him.

> They answered, "We saw clearly that the Lord was with you; so we said, 'There ought to be a sworn agreement between us'...And now you are blessed by the Lord."
> (Genesis chapter 26 verse 28 and 29)

God still has a place for you to flourish
In times of difficulty, it can easily seem that things are closing in on people and closing down. But God's plan is still in place, and this is just part of it. The obstacles in our way will bring us closer to Him, the pathway will become clearer as we walk in His footsteps, and the land, which has been prepared for us, will reap its harvest when we arrive.

God has a place where we can flourish and sometimes, we have to move and think outside of the box until we find it. This new path may seem treacherous and unsafe, but when we trust in the One who knows past, present, and future, and exists in all three, we can trust that He hasn't just abandoned us to this space with nowhere to go. God will lead us to the place where fresh water is struck, where our territory can flourish. The water in that land had been in place before Isaac arrived – they just had to dig deep to find it.

> That day Isaac's servants came and told him about the well they had dug. They said, "We've found water!"'
> (Genesis chapter 26 verse 32)

Often in tough times, we are forced to think differently, and often the thoughts that occur can be inventions or new ideas that better help those within the circumstances we are in. I'm not sure what it is that God wants you to do in these times but let me encourage you to seek Him and ask Him to show you new revelation, new ways to serve others that our old normal would not have given us thought to do.

Chapter 9

BLURRY WINDOWS

During the winter, the sun sits directly facing our front windows, highlighting the dirt that had previously gone unnoticed and reminding me of what my next job is – to clean my windows!

It's a little bit annoying. Up until now, I didn't realise how urgently those windows needed cleaning and the job hadn't been on the top of my list. Now with the light shining directly through them, I can see every speck, every smudge, the relics of earlier storms, as well as the deposits a bird or two left on their flight past.

As much as I'd like to ignore it, I can't, so on my *to-do* list this goes. The sooner they are cleaned, the better and the clearer things will be. I look forward to casting my eyes to an uninterrupted view of the colours and beauty outside without the disruption of dirty smudges in my eyeline.

Sometimes we need to shine a light on things
It's easy to carry on and ignore the dirt in our own lives. We can think we're doing everything right and forget that we may be somewhat blemished. Now, I'm not talking about forgetting to take a shower. Showers are great, but no matter how much we clean the outside of our bodies, earthly water just doesn't cut it as far as the cleanliness of our souls is concerned.

In Mark chapter seven, we read about the Pharisees questioning Jesus on one occasion when they noticed the disciples didn't wash their hands before eating. Jesus addresses this by reminding them that real dirt is what comes from the heart and is inside a person. It is this dirt which needs to be cleansed and it is not until Jesus, the Son of God, shines His light on these areas that we can truly see the dirt for what it is and be forgiven.

Sin is a bad word
These days, people don't like to mention the word 'sin'. It is confronting and people don't like to think of themselves in this way. In this day and age there is a whole gamut of pretty names given to cover over and make sins of many kinds sound harmless.

However, sin is sin, no matter which way we look at it, and it is anything but harmless. It is the same as it always has been whether we decorate it or not, and if we don't acknowledge and repent from it, we will continue to live with the weight and consequences that come with it, taking us in a direction far from where God originally intended for us.

1 John chapter 1 verses 8-10 says:

> If we claim to be without sin, we deceive ourselves and the truth is not in us. If we confess our sins, he is faithful and just and will forgive us our sins and purify us from all unrighteousness.

Without first acknowledging the sin in our lives, we miss out on the freedom and peace that comes with repentance.

Walking in the light

> …God is light; in him there is no darkness at all. If we claim to have fellowship with him and yet walk in the darkness, we lie and so not live out the truth.
>
> (1 John chapter 1 verse 6)

There is no sin in heaven for it cannot exist in the presence of a Holy God. So, for us to be free of sin and enter into the presence of the One who loves us and who has prepared a place for us, we need to acknowledge our wrongs and give them to the Saviour who paid the ultimate price once and for all.

> ... if we walk in the light, as he is in the light, we have fellowship with one another, and the blood of Jesus, his Son, purifies us from all sin.
>
> (1 John chapter 1 verse 7)

Jesus' death on the cross meant that the full punishment was taken upon Himself for what we did, making us clean and washing away our dirt, giving us a fresh start to live the best life we can in Him and opening up eternity for us. What an incredibly wonderful gift He has given us – it is truly mind-blowing!

Zechariah chapter 3 verses 3-4 says:

> Now Joshua was dressed in filthy clothes as he stood before the angel. The angel said to those who were standing before him, "Take off his filthy clothes." Then he said to Joshua, "See, I have taken away your sin, and I will put fine garments on you."

Garments of white

We can justify our actions until the cows come home, but unless we're willing to acknowledge our sin and give it up to Jesus, we're just fooling ourselves and missing out on so much.

So, it's vitally important that we let the Son shine on us regularly to reveal the things we may not want to see so that we can 'clean house'. Those windows will be much more enjoyable, and our days will capture the full colour, the full beauty, the full sense of the world around us without dirty smudges obstructing our view.

And so, we say thank you Jesus, for paying the ultimate sacrifice in giving Your life for us to have life and to have it in all its fulness, even though we don't deserve it. Such amazing love, such amazing grace!

> "Come now, let us settle the matter," says the Lord. "Though your sins are like scarlet, they shall be as white as snow; though they are red as crimson, they shall be like wool."
>
> (Isaiah chapter 1 verse 18)

Chapter 10

THE GREAT JEWEL HEIST

Some things are so valuable they would be worth breaking through a roof for. Some of you may be imagining a scene from a movie of a great jewel heist that has led to the pinnacle of the story line (after much planning, danger and drama) to arrive at the moment when the thieves have put their lives at risk and finally succeeded in surpassing all security officers, cameras and obstacles to find themselves face to face with the most priceless diamond on the face of the earth.

I'm sure we have all seen movies like this and have sat on the edge of our seats in anticipation to see if the thieves are caught in the act, or if they get away with their crime. In most cases, after all their efforts, they are caught and incarcerated, and when this happens, we're usually glad to see justice carried out.

A break-in of a different kind

Mark chapter two tells us about some men who broke in through a roof to get access to the most important gem ever to have been placed on this earth. On hearing that Jesus, the Son of God, had returned home to Capernaum, four men carried their paralysed friend on a stretcher to where He was. They were convinced that Jesus could heal him, but when they arrived at the house where Jesus was preaching, the crowds surrounding the doors and windows were beyond infiltration.

In true *Mission Impossible* style, these men were not deterred. As the old saying goes, *where there's a will there's a way!* Making their way to the roof, the four men dug through the roof until there was a hole large enough to lower the mat the man was lying on, down into the room with Jesus.

Impressive determination

I'm sure in this moment, Jesus was very impressed by these actions. I can imagine a humoured smirk on His face as He observed the efforts these men had taken to get to what they knew was a sure thing. They believed without doubt that Jesus could heal their friend and acted in full confidence of their faith.

Mark chapter 2 verse 5 says:

> When Jesus saw their faith, he said to the paralysed man, "Son, your sins are forgiven."

Then in verses 11-12:

> "I tell you, get up, take your mat and go home." He got up, took his mat and walked out in full view of them all. This amazed everyone and they praised God, saying, "We have never seen anything like this!"

Just what they expected

Though everyone else was amazed, it seems this is exactly what these four men expected to happen, otherwise they wouldn't have gone to the trouble. The faith of these men was impressive to Jesus, and so they were rewarded, and the glory of God was seen by all.

They knew who Jesus was and so they believed. The Bible tells us that:

> The kingdom of heaven is like treasure hidden in a field. When a man found it, he hid it again, and then in his joy went and sold all he had and bought that field.

> Again, the kingdom of heaven is like a merchant looking for fine pearls. When he found one of great value, he went away and sold everything he had and bought it.
>
> (Matthew chapter 13 verses 44-45)

A treasure beyond treasures
Just as the four friends knew who Jesus was and what He was capable of, reading the Word of God helps us also to understand who God is, how much He loves us and how great His power is, and this Living Word of God is the greatest treasure on earth. Unfortunately, in an age where it has never been easier for Westerners to have access to a Bible, whether in book form or on a Bible App, it can often be taken for granted that the Bible is so accessible to us, and yet, throughout the ages, many people have laid down their lives for it.

If you haven't read your Bible recently, I encourage you to dust off its cover and delve, soak and absorb yourself into this Living Word, drawing from it every understanding and revelation God gives you as the Holy Spirit begins changing your life.

I will give you hidden treasures, riches stored in secret places, so that you may know that I am the LORD, the God of Israel, who summons you by name.

(Isaiah chapter 45 verse 3)

Chapter 11

A JOB WELL DONE

Every now and then I get a glimpse of the bottom of my washing basket. It's an exciting moment and one that doesn't happen very often, but when it does, I get a tiny taste of what it might be like to have that job finished.

Unfortunately, clothes washing never really gets finished and won't unless we all decide to join a nudist colony – but that is never going to happen! So, I will just have to suck it up and try to joyfully continue to sort colours, wash, hang and fold the clothes until who knows when?

Thankfully it's not a job I hate. There is something soothing about the familiarity of it, the thinking time it gives me, and the brain-numbing monotony of doing something repeatedly that I don't have to use too much brain power for (work with me here, I'm trying to find something positive about it). After a day of problem-solving in many other areas, doing the washing can almost be (dare I say it) – therapeutic.

As a reward for my efforts, my family wears clean, nice smelling clothes which is a blessing to the noses of everyone they cross paths with. I guess you could say, this is the reaping of my sowing?

I could choose to refuse
In a household where everyone has certain jobs or chores, each job is important to the smooth running of the house. When a job fails to get done, the consequences affect everyone.

We could choose to refuse our responsibilities, but that only leads to dispute, discomfort and disharmony. To create a peaceful household, responsibilities need to be taken responsibly, and everyone benefits.

Reaping what we sow
In Galatians chapter six verse eight, Paul writes about reaping what we sow:

> Whoever sows to please their flesh, from the
> flesh will reap destruction; whoever sows to

please the Spirit, from the Spirit will reap eternal life.

Sin and righteousness also have their own results. When we live to please ourselves only, we are feeding the sinful nature and are of no fruitfulness to anyone else. By feeding our selfish desires, we take from others to make our own lives comfortable – which funnily enough, has the opposite result and ends up making us uncomfortable.

When we live to edify and build others up by allowing the Spirit to flow through us, we see the fruits at work reaping a bountiful harvest and filling us with greater joy than we could ever have imagined.

Made for more
Obviously, I am no longer talking specifically about washing, but if we take a simple concept like that, it sometimes helps to put other areas of our lives into perspective.

God doesn't want us to be islands working only for our own pleasure. We were made for more than that, and when we all work together for the good of each other, we create a beautiful world and joy comes bounding back to us.

> Let us not become weary in doing good, for at the proper time we will reap a harvest if we do not give up. Therefore, as we have opportunity, let us do good to all people, especially to those who belong to the family of believers.
>
> (Galatians chapter 6 verses 9-10)

So, while jobs like doing washing or taking the bins out, may seem menial and insignificant, it's good to take heed of the old saying which says, *don't put off to tomorrow what could be done today.*

Though sometimes I prefer to say, *I'm putting off until tomorrow what could be done today because today has enough troubles of its own* (on second thoughts… maybe don't follow that one).

POEM

THE SCRIBE

She wrote the words with special care,
A careful scribe yet unaware.
The words took meaning of their own,
And fluttered out beyond their home.

They followed up a windy path
To where a toddler took a bath,
And while her mother read them well
The words within began to dwell.

A fairy princess on her horse,
A castle high on distant shores
Captured her imagination,
Filled her with anticipation.

To another floated by
The words of wonders of the sky,
Of flying birds and soaring planes,
Of battling skies and roaring trains.

Yet to another something special,
Words of comfort, calm and settled,
Soothing to a wounded heart,
Where light begins to break the dark.

And yet, she wrote beyond her pen,
Of where and what? would now depend
On where the flowing breeze would blow,
Where they would land, she did not know.

And we know that in all things God works for the good of those who love him, who have been called according to his purpose.

(Romans 8:28)

Chapter 12

SMALL BEGINNINGS ARE FULL OF SURPRISES

"Mum, do you think you could teach me how to play the guitar?" asked my eleven-year-old son one day after school. I had played a little guitar when in school and remembered a beginners guitar book that was sitting in our music room.

"Sure, give me a minute and we'll go have a look," I replied. We began by tuning the guitar as best we could and slowly worked through the fingering of the first chord. By the end of his first amateur lesson with me, Benaton's fingers were sore, but he had found enough desire to learn this instrument, and he would return to the guitar every spare moment for years to come.

Now, a few years on, he is a prolific guitar player performing regularly in a band that he formed, as well as regularly playing in the church worship band. His whole world revolves around his gift of music which began with playing the drums since he was big enough to hold the sticks, and as he plans his career course, I know his future is going to revolve around music as well.

When I think of that very first lesson, as elementary as it was on my end, I am astounded at what those small beginnings turned into. I really didn't have a lot I could teach him, yet it was enough to get him started. Needless to say, I wasn't his guitar teacher for more than two or three lessons, for he quickly surpassed my limited guitar knowledge and today I am the proud mum and number one fan (along with our family), cheering him on whenever he performs.

Don't despise the day of small things
Reading through the prophets in the Old Testament, you can feel God's excitement as the time to rebuild His temple was coming closer. The LORD decreed that it would begin, and though it was delayed and took time, He says, in Zechariah chapter four verse ten:

> Who dares despise the day of small things, since the seven eyes of the LORD that range throughout the earth will rejoice when they see the chosen capstone in the hand of Zerubbabel?

God didn't see just a capstone; He saw the completed result before it even began. It was in His heart and, being God, time has no boundary to Him, therefore, He knew the completion of the work would come to be because He was also already there.

Though there may be mountains in our way in the form of obstacles and trials, God speaks and says:

> What are you, mighty mountain? Before Zerubbabel you will become level ground. Then he will bring out the capstone to shouts of 'God bless it! God bless it!'
> (Zechariah chapter 4 verse 7)

You can feel His excitement!

Purpose in our lives

When God puts a plan and a purpose on each one of our lives, He is excited at its beginnings because He knows what it will be and will see it through to its completion. I kind of see His excitement as that of a parent on Christmas Eve; you know the gifts your child will open the next morning and you are excited for what is coming to them, but you have to let them open them up and discover it for themselves.

God is excited for the purpose and plans He has given to each one of us. We may think that what we are doing isn't very important or is overwhelming because we're just at the beginning and are wondering if it will even work.

If God has placed something on your heart, then He will carry it on to completion, we just have to keep going. When only the foundation of the temple had been laid, God spoke and said,

> The hands of Zerubbabel have laid the foundation of this temple; his hands will also complete it. Then you will know that the LORD Almighty has sent me to you.
> (Zechariah chapter 4 verse 9)

When God gives us a mighty task, He knows its completion will point to Him. He doesn't want us to give up halfway. He doesn't want us to look at the beginning of something great and say, "Oh, it's too hard! I don't think I can do anymore on that." Though you may be right to say it's too hard, when God puts great things on our hearts, it's in His strength that He wants us to complete it.

> So he said to me, "This is the word of the LORD to Zerubbabel: 'Not by might nor by power, but by my Spirit,'" says the LORD Almighty.
>
> (Zechariah chapter 4 verse 6)

Of course, you can't do it on your own

More often than not, we can't do it on our own and that's the point. Faith means leaning into God. It means, needing Him and knowing that we can't do it ourselves, but we certainly can do all things through Christ who strengthens us. Which is the point really. The glory must always go back to the Father, the great and Sovereign God who makes us fly on wings like eagles.

And if you're feeling unworthy, remember, He takes the unlikely ones to shine His glory through. 1 Corinthians chapter 1 verses 26-31 says:

> Brothers and sisters, think of what you were when you were called. Not many of you were wise by human standards; not many were influential; not many were of noble birth. But God chose the foolish things of the world to shame the wise; God chose the weak things of the world to shame the strong. God chose the lowly things of this

> world and the despised things – and the things that are not – to nullify the things that are, so that no one may boast before him. It is because of him that you are in Christ Jesus, who has become for us wisdom from God – that is, our righteousness, holiness and redemption. Therefore, as it is written: "Let the one who boasts boast in the Lord."

God knew all along that my son would pursue a calling to music, for that is what was put inside of him when he was created. If I didn't take the time to encourage that moment of teaching, I'm sure he would have found it some other way. I am just glad that I did, and that we share that special memory together. Who knows what God has planned for his future? Only time will tell, but boy, I am sure going to enjoy the show and will always remember those precious 'small beginnings'.

Chapter 13

DON'T LET YOUR GOD-FRAGRANCE END UP IN THE BELLY OF A GOAT

Seven was the number of white rose standards planted down my driveway before I went to sleep. Three is number of rose standards left with roses on them after our pet goat escaped in the middle of the night to devour them.

A goat having a midnight feast on my roses was not what I expected to see when I happened to peek out of the window after waking at midnight. While I was thankful that I saw him when I did, I'm not sure my husband was completely thankful at having to chase the goat in the middle of the night, followed by me running up the driveway in my pyjamas, ready to corner the goat if he escaped while my husband fixed the fence.

It was sad to wake bleary-eyed in the morning to see the missing white roses that had beautifully framed that part of our garden. As my eyes drifted from the bare rose bushes to the fenced area of our animals, I noticed the goat was still sleeping with a full belly and looking very satisfied. He had no appreciation for those beautiful roses except for filling his tummy.

While I considered again what goat curry might taste like, I thought about what a thing of beauty those roses had been to our visitors and to us over the past weeks, and how the fragrance and beauty of those roses would no longer be appreciated, as they were no longer visible for the senses to enjoy (that is until the next ones grow).

Using the gifts we have been given
God gives each of us wonderful gifts. Even if we don't realise it, we have been given gifts for the enjoyment and service of others.

1 Peter chapter 4 verses 10-11 says:

> Each of you should use whatever gift you have received to serve others, as faithful stewards of God's grace in its various forms. If anyone speaks, they should do so as one who speaks the very words of God. If anyone

serves, they should do so with the strength God provides, so that in all things God may be praised through Jesus Christ. To him be the glory and the power for ever and ever. Amen.

Though we may all have been given gifts, not all of us use them. Whether it be from fear, shyness, doubt, laziness, or whatever, there are all sorts of reasons we talk ourselves out of not being as effective as what we perhaps should be and therefore, our gifts may as well be sitting in the belly of a goat.

Personal challenge
I was recently personally challenged on this. I was struggling with going more public on social media. I felt that it was too brash and didn't want to appear prideful or to be promoting myself. I was comfortable with my limited online presence and also liked the amount of anonymity I had in choosing what I wanted to share and when I wanted to share it.

Then God challenged me. Throughout the course of a few weeks, God showed me that, if we are to reach the world with His good news of salvation, we need to use whatever platform He has made available to us and share it. He showed me that I was not being humble by wanting to shrink into the shadows, but rather – I was being selfish.

I was being selfish because the message God wanted me to share was about Him – and if I didn't do what I felt God was compelling me to do, I was actually being disobedient. It was time to step out of my comfort zone and trust God with the next steps.

> It is written: "I believed; therefore I have spoken." Since we have that same spirit of faith, we also believe and therefore speak, because we know that the one who raised the Lord Jesus from the dead will also raise us with Jesus and present us with you to himself.
> (2 Corinthians chapter 4 verses 13-14)

When we hide things

Matthew chapter 25 verses 14 to 30 tells us a story about a property owner who was going on a journey and entrusted his property to his servants while he was gone.

> To one he gave five talents, another two, to another one, to each according to his ability. Then he went away. (verse 15)

While he was gone, each invested their talents in different ways gaining good returns on their investments and were generously rewarded – except for the servant who received one talent. He buried his talent in the ground where it did not even make interest, and so his one talent was taken away from him and he was cast into the darkness.

Sometimes fear and doubt get in the way of the wonderful things God has for both the giver and the receiver, giving the enemy a foothold over our lives – and there is no happy ending to that.

John chapter 10 verse 10 says:

> The thief comes only to steal and kill and destroy. I came that they may have life and have it abundantly.

The abundant life God has for us is free from fear and doubt. We are not to be lazy with our gifts but instead we are compelled to use them, to be bold and to be joyful with it.

> Do not be slothful in zeal, be fervent in spirit, serve the Lord.
> (Romans chapter 12 verse 11)

A pleasant fragrance

Just as the fragrance of my beautiful roses had been enjoyed by those who saw them, we too are like a fragrance, spreading to those who hear it as we carry the message of Christ's forgiveness to the ends of the earth.

> But thanks be to God, who always leads us as captives in Christ's triumphal procession and uses us to spread the aroma of the knowledge of him everywhere. For we are to God the pleasing aroma of Christ among those who are perishing. To the one we are an aroma that brings death; to the other an aroma that brings life.
> (2 Corinthians chapter 2 verses 14-16)

Let's not be shy in using our gifts to promote the *Good News*. Allow your fragrance to spread far and wide – and not end up in the belly of a goat.

Chapter 14

WHERE THERE IS LIGHT THERE IS HOPE

I used to be incredibly afraid of the dark. So much so, that for years as a child I would need to have the lamp on all night while I slept and if anyone turned it off, I would become frighteningly scared of what I could not see.

When I was about seven or eight years old, I prayed about this debilitating fear that I'd had and God, in His great kindness and love, answered me through a verse in the Bible:

> "I am the light of the world. Whoever follows me will never walk in darkness, but will have the light of life."
> (John chapter 8 verse 12)

Suddenly, a light turned on for me! (excuse the pun – I couldn't help it). I ran to my mum and proudly proclaimed, "Mum! I'm not afraid of the dark anymore."

She was very surprised, as this had been something that I had battled with every night for years. I explained that I'd read the verse in the Bible, and it dawned on me that if Jesus is the light of the world, and He lives in me – then I have the light with me all the time! *He* is the light in my room.

It was an epiphany, and my parents were amazed at how God had spoken to my heart so strongly with this understanding. It was an immediate fix, and I never needed to leave the lamp on at night again.

Increasing darkness

Things have certainly changed in the last few years. The world that we live in today can look very dark. There are wars and rumours of wars. There are corrupt governments oppressing their own people. There are sicknesses and pestilences that the Bible talks about already being seen.

In the political space, I have had the privilege to talk to many people on these topics and the same concern is being voiced over and over again, "Where is this all going to end?"

One thing we know is if things keep travelling along this trajectory, it could end very badly, and according to the book of Revelation, ultimately it will for many – but not yet. While the light is still in the world, there is hope. While the world may look dark, God reminds us that He has not yet removed the light. In fact, the light is growing!

> As long as it is day, we must do the works of him who sent me. Night is coming, when no one can work. While I am in the world, I am the light of the world.
>
> (John chapter 9 verse 4)

For those of us who are in Christ, we have been given the gift of the Holy Spirit who dwells within us – the promised helper. If God is within us in the form of the Holy Spirit, then we carry the light and are the light of the world.

> You are the light of the world. A town built on a hill cannot be hidden. Neither do people light a lamp and put it under a bowl. Instead they put it on its stand, and it gives

> light to everyone in the house. In the same way, let your light shine before others, that they may see your good deeds and glorify your Father in heaven.
>
> (Matthew chapter 5 verses 14-16)

Don't be afraid

We do not need to be afraid of what we cannot see in the dark, for God can see it, knows it all, and is illuminating what is in the darkness for all to see. While the light is exposing what was once hidden, it is the unveiling that must take place to bring into account what has been wrong. What we are seeing is the 'great revealing' or 'revelation'. Jesus says in Matthew chapter 10 verse 26:

> So do not be afraid of them, for there is nothing concealed that will not be disclosed, or hidden that will not be made known.

It is certainly comforting to know that nothing is hidden from the sight of our Heavenly Father and that He is bringing all things into conformity under Him.

God loves light because He is light. When He created the world, the first thing He said was, "Let there be light!" (Genesis chapter 1 verse 3). So as the song says, let us live in the light as He is in the light. Let us shine like the stars in the heavens.

Therefore, take courage and remember that He who is in you is greater than he who is in the world. Let your light shine so that others may see your good deeds.

> … The people living in darkness have seen a great light; on those living in the land of the shadow of death a light has dawned.
> (Matthew chapter 4 verses 15-17)

Chapter 15

STOP CRYING AND LAUGH

The funeral had concluded, and the hearse slowly and respectfully drove out of the church parking bay and onto the road. Onlookers were likely shocked to see what appeared to be family members standing on the road behind the moving hearse, hurling their fists and choice words at the remains of the dearly departed soul being transported to their final resting place.

One would think they were glad to see the back of them – that whatever grievances they'd had with this person, they were not afraid to show it publicly – bidding them good riddance!

As I stood giggling at this strange scene before me, I felt that my recently departed grandmother would have been secretly proud of her daughters hurling abuse as she left in the hearse; for it was not her that they were hurling abuse at. Seconds earlier, a car had sped down the road cutting off the hearse in its path while beeping its horn, and what appeared to be family disharmony, was actually family uniting.

With all good intentions, my aunties united, standing on the road, fists in the air, to let this so-and-so know exactly how rude they were to do this in such a sombre and sad moment. Very quickly the sombre moment became a very funny scene, and it felt good to stop crying and laugh.

Stop crying and laugh
Have you ever felt that feeling when something is so ridiculous you just have to laugh? When things go from bad to worse, but it suddenly becomes funny? I know I have, and perhaps it sounds like madness, but I think both emotions of grief and humour can sometimes be very closely knit.

Abram and Sarai in the Bible knew exactly how that felt. Abram was 99 years old and his wife Sarai was 90 years old when God appeared to them with good news.

They were finally going to have a baby! Imagine waiting almost 100 years for the promise of a child. Sarai would have born the scorn of a barren woman for years, despite her husband's good standing and wealth. But God had a plan beyond what is humanly possible – a plan that would bring glory to Him.

New assignments, new beginnings
In God's perfect timing, He appeared to them, changed their names to Abraham and Sarah, and anointed them with a new assignment. The past had gone and the new was beginning. They had waited a very long time and proven steadfast in their faith, and now they were to be entrusted with the honour of being the parents of a multitude of nations that would continue for all time – a multitude that would start with one baby.

Both of them laughed. I could imagine the laughter was one of amazement, joy and incredible relief that the moment had arrived, as well as being flabbergasted at the incredulity of the logistics of such a feat. It was one of those moments where their capacity to wait had been pushed beyond what was humanly possible. Sarah was beyond her years to bear children so, despite knowing that God was fully capable and able to do this, it brought about one response – laughter!

When God announced this to Abraham, he fell on his face and laughed (Genesis chapter 17 verse 17). When Sarah heard what God had said, she also laughed.

Genesis chapter 21 verses 5-6 says:

> Abraham was a hundred years old when his son Isaac was born to him. And Sarah said, "God has made laughter for me; everyone who hears will laugh over me." And she said, "Who would have said to Abraham that Sarah would nurse children? Yet I have borne him a son in his old age."

Joy will come in the morning

When God says He will do something, He will do it. Sometimes we can feel like prisoners of hope, waiting in our promises for what feels at times like an eternity. But if God said it, then the day will certainly come. We have important work to do in the meantime and while we wait, we are to live like we're preparing for the promise.

Zechariah chapter 9 verse 12 puts it like this:

> Return to your fortress, you prisoners of hope; even now I announce that I will restore twice as much to you.

Even if it seems impossible in human understanding, even if we have outlasted our capacity of waiting, even if we're on the last strands of hope – God will come through because He is faithful.

And when He does, there will be joy. Where we once wept, we will laugh and be glad. When our hearts were once heavy, they will be light. And just as the appearance of my aunties yelling at my grandmother's hearse could have been misconstrued as something else, the appearance of our circumstances, as dire as they seem, may soon turn in an instant and lead to joy.

Psalm 126

> When the LORD restored the fortunes of Zion,
> We were like those who dreamed.
> Our mouths were filled with laughter,
> Our tongues with songs of joy.
> Then it was said among the nations,
> "The LORD has done great things for them."
> The LORD has done great things for us,
> And we are filled with joy.
> Restore our fortunes, LORD,
> Like streams in the Negev.

Those who sow with tears will reap with songs of joy.
Those who go out weeping, carrying seed to sow, will return with songs of joy, carrying sheaves with them.

POEM

HER HOME BEYOND THE RIVER

He led her down the winding stairs
To where? It was unknown.
And then across the paddock green,
Oh, how the wind did blow.
She stopped upon a garden bed
Where yellow flowers grew,
And whispered in the open air,
"I wish I had known you."

Then caught up in a torrent rush,
The Apple Berries stomped to mush,
And in a flurry hurried much,
To see the distant treasure.
And if she just once caught it by,
And in a moment not so shy,
The hurried years now rushing by,
Were seen beyond a measure.

And as she stopped to take her breath,
The flying colours in her head,
The captured essence in her stead,
So quick it gave a shiver.
The ragged mulling up ahead,
And gentle though the evening tread,
She knew to where her home had led,
Her home beyond the river.

You have made my days a mere handbreadth;
the span of my years is as nothing before you.
Everyone is but a breath,
even those who seem secure.
(Psalm 39:5)

Chapter 16

LIGHT BULB MOMENTS

One of my sons has entered his senior years at school and it has suddenly dawned on him that the work they are given during the term lessons, is to equip them for their assessments at the end of the term.

"I noticed," he said, "because the teacher kept telling us to take note of these things as it will be on our assessment task. I always just thought they gave us boring work during the term to fill in the time until assessment time."

Finally! Thank you Jesus! A very important light-bulb moment and maybe just in time to make his senior years successful. Now that he's had this epiphany, I have never seen him more motivated to achieve in his studies. It would have been great if this had occurred to him earlier, but hey – better late than never!

Light-bulb moments

When something suddenly dawns on us, it really is quite an enlightening moment, which is probably why we call them 'light-bulb moments'. It's like someone just turned on a light to see clearly what was hiding in the dark, or what we were even unaware was there.

Reading the book of Haggai in the Old Testament of the Bible, the Jews also had somewhat of a light-bulb moment. They had returned from exile in Babylon to Jerusalem and had rebuilt their houses with panelled walls, yet they would plant but harvest little, eat but never have enough, drink but never have their fill. They would put on clothes, but not be warm, earn wages only to put them in a purse with holes in it (Haggai chapter 1 verse 6).

The Lord spoke at the time through a prophet named Haggai and told them to give careful thought to their ways. He highlighted these problems they were having, which they probably weren't fully aware of until it was brought to their attention.

> "You expected much, but see, it turned out to be little. What you brought home, I blew away. Why?" declares the LORD Almighty.

> "Because of my house, which remains a ruin, while each of you is busy with your own house."
>
> (Haggai chapter 1 verse 9)

A face palming moment

I can almost imagine the people face palming themselves in realisation, saying, "Of course! How did we not see that?"

While the Jews had been focussed on building their own richly decorated houses, they had left the house of God in ruins.

Thank goodness God cared enough to bring it to their attention. Once they realised what they had been doing, the hearts of the people received what the Lord had said, and they turned their hearts and minds to rebuilding the house of God.

Sometimes we can get caught up in doing our own thing, working hard, only to struggle through finding enough for each day, (or in my son's case, getting to the end of each school day). These times can be seasons of trusting in God to provide, but it's also a good idea to stop now and then and consider where our focus lies.

Though we may not have to physically build a church or building to bring glory to God, are we living our lives in a way that our attention and focus is bringing attention and glory to God? Are we building God's kingdom through the way we interact with people, through the way we do business, through the way we study, through the way that we parent our children?

Consider what God did for the Jews once they returned their focus onto Him. He declared that He was with them, and stirred up the spirits of Zerubbabel, governor of Judah, the spirit of Joshua, and the spirit of the whole remnant of the people, and they began to work together on the house of the Lord Almighty, their God (Haggai chapter 1 verses 13-14).

He made them this promise:

> "The glory of this present house will be greater than the glory of the former house," says the LORD Almighty. "And in this place I will grant peace," declares the LORD Almighty.
>
> (Haggai chapter 2 verse 9)

Churches have gone through great transitions in recent times, and my prayer is that God will stir up the spirits of His people as we have light-bulb moments and turn our eyes and hearts and minds and souls onto Him. And may the glory of this present house be greater than the glory of the former house as we look for guidance as we rebuild.

> Unless the LORD builds the house, the builders labour in vain. Unless the LORD watches over the city, the guards stand watch in vain.
> In vain you rise early and stay up late, toiling for food to eat—for he grants sleep to those he loves.
>
> (Psalm chapter 127 verses 1-2)

Chapter 17

DO YOU HEAR THE PEOPLE SING?

When I was a little girl, I loved going to Sunday school and singing the songs our teachers taught us. Little did I know that these songs would stay with me my whole life and come back at just the right moments. One song that has been playing in my mind recently has been the following. I wonder if you remember it.

> Give me oil in my lamp keep me burning,
> Give me oil in my lamp I pray,
> Give me oil in my lamp keep me burning,
> Keep me burning till the break of day.
>
> Sing Hosanna! Sing Hosanna!
> Sing Hosanna to the King of Kings (rpt)

Hosanna in the Bible means 'to save' and is used as a shout of jubilation to the One who saves – our Saviour. He is coming soon, and we need to be ready.

Sing!

On a wall in our house where a series of Scriptures are hung, I again see the word 'Sing!'

> Sing, Daughter Zion;
> Shout aloud, Israel!
> Be glad and rejoice with all your heart, Daughter Jerusalem!
> The LORD has taken away your punishment, he has turned back your enemy.
> The LORD, the King of Israel, is with you;
> never again will you fear any harm.
>
> On that day they will say to Jerusalem,
> "Do not fear, Zion;
> do not let your hands hang limp.
> The LORD your God is with you,
> the Mighty Warrior who saves.
> He will take great delight in you;
> in his love he will no longer rebuke you,
> but will rejoice over you with singing."
>
> (Zephaniah chapter 3 verses 14-17)

It seems that while the world is shouting "Be very afraid!" God, the one who saves, is shouting "Sing! And be glad!" and I feel a bubbling of joy rise up within me. It's like a clash of the clans but I know which voice I love to listen to, and I know why He is saying "Daughter, Sing!"

Numbered days

You see, the days of the enemy are numbered. His days are coming to a swift end, and he is trying to drag as many people down with him as possible. But for the children of God, and those who are yet to be part of God's family, our future looks bright! So bright that even though the world may seem to get darker, God's light is getting brighter and is becoming unmistakably glorious to all who look for Him, and to Him. God's glory will shine throughout the earth as the days till His return grow ever so close.

It is really rather exciting. We know we are victorious because we are on the winning team. Our eyes are not to humankind who breed fear and uncertainty; no, our eyes are on God who knows the present, past and the future – and the future is bright for we are not of this world, but of the world to come.

> But our citizenship is in heaven. And we eagerly await a Saviour from there, the Lord Jesus Christ, who, by the power that enables him to bring everything under his control, will transform our lowly bodies so that they will be like his glorious body.
> (Philippians chapter 3 verses 20-21)

You can read about it in His Word, the Bible. He knows how it ends, and the end is actually the beginning.

If you are finding that you are leaning more towards the fear of man rather than the fear of God, turn off your radios and turn to the Word.

> The fear of the LORD leads to life; then one rests content, untouched by trouble.
> (Proverbs chapter 19 verse 23)

> Then he opened their minds so they could understand the Scriptures.
> (Luke chapter 24 verse 47)

Chapter 18

UP THE CREEK WITHOUT A PADDLE

Many years ago, we visited my parents while holidaying at a small seaside town in Queensland. While there, we spent the afternoon by the bay. We all enjoyed a leisurely spring afternoon swim, and towards sunset, my mum decided to go for a relaxing row in the dinghy by herself.

With the outgoing tide, it wasn't long before she was a fair way out. Dad was keeping an eye on her, and she seemed like she was having a great time, until we realised she was calling out to us. She was quite frantic by this stage. Apparently, she had been calling for some time, but because she was so far away, we couldn't hear her – we just thought she was waving.

Apparent trouble
Her paddling didn't seem to be doing much, and with the sun beginning to set, she was getting worried. The boat was being drawn further and further out and Mum was not able to direct the boat back into shore.

As she sat in the boat calling for help, not daring to stand up incase she fell into the water, she couldn't believe her eyes when the men of our family began walking out to her – seemingly on water! When they arrived at the boat, they said, *"Jenny, get out of the boat and walk."* Incredible! This must be a miracle!

What she hadn't realised, however, was that there was a long sandbar that reached all the way out as far as she had rowed, and at any time, she could have stepped out of the boat and pulled it back to shore.

As funny as it was, it got me thinking. Sometimes in life, we are thrust into difficult situations and our first inclination is to fret. *"Help! We're all going to die!"* (Or maybe not to that extreme).

With Christ in my vessel…
Matthew chapter 8 verses 23-27 tells us about a time when Jesus sailed with the disciples in a boat. A great storm arose on the sea, so violent that the boat was

being swamped by the waves and the disciples were in fear for their lives.

While the turmoil happened all around them, Jesus slept. Completely peaceful. When He was woken by the fear-stricken disciples, He asked why they were afraid? After all, God in human form was in the boat with them!

Jesus, having full authority over everything, 'rebuked the winds and the sea, and there was great calm' (verse 26).

I was reminded lately of a song from my childhood, you may remember it:

> With Christ in my vessel I can smile at the storm, smile at the storm, smile at the storm… as we go sailing home.

This was the entirety of the lyrics for the song, but I believe there is a reason for that. When you think about who Christ is – the Powerful, Almighty, Sovereign, Saviour, Redeemer, Creator, Everlasting Father, Maker of heaven and earth, Creator of all life…and I could go on and on – when we remember who He Is, then why do we ever need to worry?

For when Jesus rose to heaven, He sent His Spirit to dwell within us, so we literally have the Spirit of Christ within our vessel – within us!

Just ponder on that for – well, forever. I'm not even sure how completely our minds can appreciate or comprehend this wonderful gift we have been given. At least in part to begin with, then increasingly as it is revealed. But if we can grasp it, if we can understand that the presence of God is within us, how wonderful and powerful the people of God would be on this earth!

Jesus says in John chapter 14 verses 12-14:

> Very truly I tell you, whoever believes in me will do the works I have been doing, and they will do even greater things than these, because I am going to the Father. And I will do whatever you ask in my name, so that the Father may be glorified in the Son. You may ask me for anything in my name, and I will do it.

So, next time you feel the waves crashing in around you, remember: With Christ in my vessel, I can smile at the storm! He's got a plan, He has the power, and all we need to do is ask – He is able to calm the storm.

POEM

BE STILL

Be still my ears and listen.
To the rustling of the leaves,
The breeze it flows straight through the boughs
And quickly disappears.

Be still my eyes and notice.
The sky is silent grey,
The clouds sit heavy hanging,
It is the end of day.

Be still my heart and listen.
The thunder rumbles by,
The soft sweet sound of distant birds,
Their shelter still to find.

Be still my mind and rest,
And let your thoughts be kind.
Now settle in the evening dusk,
Give way to the Divine.

He says, "Be still and know that I am God; I will be exalted among the nations, I will be exalted in the earth."

(Psalm 46:10)

Chapter 19

WHEN THE CUP IS FULL

Some seasons of life are busier than others. Sometimes our cups are full and not necessarily in the negative sense. They can be full of good things, but even a cup full of good things needs careful handling.

When life is busy and there is no room left in that cup to fit anything else, distractions and unexpected demands such as car troubles, unexpected bills, extra demands on time, and changes in weather (like when you are planning an outdoor event and it's raining), amongst other things, have the potential to overflow that cup and you find yourself juggling to catch what's falling out the top!

Negative distractions can sap us of any energy we may have left, cause us to worry, and affect our health. But there are ways to deal with this and I am learning new skills as I go along.

Throw it forward

It's times like these I like to take a little step back and throw myself into the future, picturing everything as being done and looking back on the season being a success. Will I want to remember these times as a time of stress, mess, and exhaustion? Definitely not. I will want my memories to be of a beautiful season of life, where love, warmth, and celebration triumph above all.

To ensure my memories are that of the latter, I need to take authority over the little 'foxes' trying to cause distraction and havoc in what should be a lovely time. To do this, I am learning three main points which are very beneficial to coping.

1. Deal with what can be dealt with promptly. When unexpected problems crop up, they are best dealt with quickly and promptly. Sometimes this is not possible, but time spent correcting things that may otherwise sit heavy on the heart, take up space in our minds, or sap time and energy, is worth doing to preserve energy that will be needed for later.

2. Take your mind off what can't be dealt with and give your attention to better things. When we focus on worries, it only weighs us down. God tells us throughout the Bible not to worry about anything, instead we are to focus on what is good. In Philippians chapter 4 verse 8, Paul tells us:

> …whatever is pure, whatever is lovely, whatever is admirable—if anything is excellent or praiseworthy—think about such things.

And in verse seven he explains that it is the 'peace of God' that will guard your hearts and your minds in Christ Jesus.

3. Keep your eye on the prize, keep your goals on track. Paul tells us again in Philippians chapter 3 verses 12-14:

> "Not that I have already obtained all this, or have already arrived at my goal, but I press on to take hold of that for which Christ Jesus took hold of me. Brothers and sisters, I do not consider myself yet to have taken hold of it. But one thing I do: Forgetting what is behind and straining toward what is ahead, I press on toward the goal to win the prize for which God has called me heavenward in Christ Jesus."

In all these things, the most important thing is to stay close to God and remember that Jesus walks with us through the good and the bad. We can talk to Him about everything along the way and when we seek Him first, He gives us solutions, parts the waters, and gives us peace and joy. And joy is what we need to take with us on any journey. So, breathe, relax, and trust God. He will make the way.

> Nehemiah said, "Go and enjoy choice food and sweet drinks, and send some to those who have nothing prepared. This day is holy to our Lord. Do not grieve, for the joy of the LORD is your strength."
>
> (Nehemiah chapter 8 verse 10)

Chapter 20

THE GREAT ROAR!

If you have little children, have you ever noticed how quickly they can slip out of your grasp and out of your site? I remember a specific time when my children were little, and I took them shopping to buy some clothes for winter. With them right by my side, I looked away for just a few seconds, but when I looked back, one was gone.

Immediately my mind went to the worst possible scenario. *Someone had obviously taken my son and was now walking out of the shops towards the carpark, and I would never see him again!* My heart and imagination went into over-drive, and I made a bee-line straight for the shop front doors in order to overtake the perpetrator, who I planned to tackle to the ground until he let go of my son and then I would make a citizen's arrest alerting everyone in the shopping centre to this callous person's actions and what they'd tried to do.

My beeline, however, was cut short by an all too familiar giggle coming from underneath one of the clothing racks followed by an almighty *"Roar!"* as my son jumped forward to surprise me, laughing the entire time at his successful trick.

You're all feeling it with me right now aren't you… should I hug him or be cranky with him? Let's just say my reaction was a bit of both, but overall, it was one of great relief! And the experience was enough to make me want to leave for the safety of home much sooner than I had planned.

Take a breath
Things aren't always as they seem, and though our imaginations often get the better of us, it is good to know that we are often wrong.

When Jesus died on the cross, appearances showed that Jesus' life had ended; the enemy thought he had succeeded in killing the Son of God. How wrong he was! First appearances showed this to be true as Jesus hung on the cross beaten and bloodied, but God had other plans.

While this was all happening, Jesus was dealing with death, once and for all, and making a spectacular *"ROAR!"* in the spiritual realm, defeating the enemy in order for all of God's children to come to Him and receive eternal life.

Circumstances can sometimes seem dire in the natural and the enemy takes delight in seeing people scared and fearful. But God says repeatedly throughout the Bible, *"Do not fear!"*

Fear only gives power to evil, while faith gives way to miracles. We know the God in whom we trust, and we know that He is able to do *'immeasurably more than we can ask or imagine'* (Ephesians chapter 3 verse 20).

While the natural appears one way, God's plan is abundantly more elaborate, and He is at work all the time. At just the right time He will make a *"ROAR!"* and reveal the perfection of the goodness of God, revealing His great plan. How exciting! The question is, which scenario has our focus? The good scenario or the worst?

God is doing greater things
Just like a little child who is afraid of the dark or a storm or a spider, instincts bring them straight into

the arms of the one they find safety in. They throw their arms around you and tuck themselves under your arms for safety and refuge. In turn, our arms wrap around them, and we utter words of comfort and reassurance that all will be well. We know we are capable of keeping them safe and capable to deal with the danger at hand due to our greater understanding of the situation.

So too, God is our great Father who covers us with His feathers, and under whose wings we will find refuge (Psalm chapter 91 verse 4).

Psalm chapter 5 verse 11 says:

> ...let all who take refuge in you be glad; let them sing for joy. Spread your protection over them, that those who love your name may rejoice in you.

God wants us to come to Him like a little child, wrapping our arms around His waist while He covers us in His. When things may seem unsure or unsettling in the natural, remember – God's plans are greater. He is the source of life and healing and comfort. He has many surprises in store for us and, if we make our refuge in

Him, He will reveal them at just the right time, and we will celebrate in the great and triumphant *"ROAR!"* of our God.

Chapter 21

THERE'S MORE TO YOUR PAIN THAN MEETS THE EYE

When I think about some very tough times I've been through that, at the time, didn't feel like they would ever end (read chapter 25, *Are we there yet,* from my book *First to Forty*), I remember, in the midst of my trouble, reading Psalm chapter 30 verse 5: '…weeping may stay for the night, but rejoicing comes in the morning.'

Oh, how I longed for that morning to come! Verses like these are what I clung to in those moments. It was these verses that gave me hope in the gravest of circumstances even though, at the time, I had no idea when that morning would come – or if it ever would.

Hope

We don't always understand why we have to go through difficult things. At the time, it may make no sense and feel like there is no way out. When we feel like this, there is often a temptation to give up, to cower in the difficulty of the moment, or to cry out to God and ask "Why?"

Is it actually ours to know why everything happens? Though we don't know why, God does, and as we get through to the other side of the trials, and even a few years down the track – we may even find ourselves thanking God for it! Sounds crazy I know. Why would we thank God for things that caused us great pain, turmoil and loss?

The first thing we have to acknowledge is that we will *get* through it, but first we have to *go* through it. Often, we will feel like we are being broken during these times, and often we are. But there is beauty in brokenness.

Peter

In Luke chapter 22, we see the disciples sitting with Jesus at the last supper. For some reason, they began disputing who among them was considered to be the greatest. Not long after Jesus settled that matter by explaining that the greatest in the kingdom of God must have the heart of a servant, He turned to Simon Peter and said:

> Simon, Simon, Satan has asked to sift all of you as wheat. But I have prayed for you, Simon, that your faith may not fail. And when you have turned back, strengthen your brothers.
>
> (Luke chapter 22 verses 31-32)

These are very profound and revelatory pieces of information Jesus is giving Simon Peter (also known as Peter) at this point in time. Peter didn't fully understand just yet, but he was about to go through some severe testing.

Testing times

Peter replied, *"Lord, I am ready to go with you to prison and to death."* Jesus responds to Peter and reveals that Peter would, indeed, deny Him three times by the time the rooster crowed. Obviously, Peter thought this was not possible – he loved Jesus very much.

Knowing all that was about to take place, Jesus also warned the disciples to pray so that they would not fall into temptation. Part of this temptation was, of course, that Satan had asked to *'sift the disciples as wheat'* and Peter would be tempted to deny Jesus.

God allows testing for our good
What is amazing here is that, when Satan asked God if he could *'sift the disciples as wheat'*, Jesus steps in and prays on their behalf. But He does not pray for this to be stopped. He knew, in His greater knowledge and wisdom, that though this would be a time of testing for them, the outcome would reap great benefits for generations right throughout time from that moment to now.

You see Peter had the choice in the events to come, of how to respond, yet the response he chose was one he would greatly regret later. God still used it for good.

Jesus' prayer for Simon Peter was not that this trial be taken from him, but that his *'faith would not fail'* and that when he has turned back, he would strengthen his brothers (v.32).

Why did Jesus not just pray that they be protected from this trial and that God would reject Satan's request? Because Jesus knew that greater blessing would come from this trial, and greater faith would be developed in Peter which he was going to need for the rest of his life in ministry.

Failure hurts

When Peter realised that he had denied Jesus three times when the rooster crowed,

> The Lord turned and looked straight at Peter. Then Peter remembered the word the Lord had spoken to him "Before the rooster crows today, you will disown me three times." And he went outside and wept bitterly.
> (Luke chapter 22 verses 61-62)

Simon Peter's anguish at betraying Jesus spurred on his faith to be stronger than ever before. Great forgiveness spurs on great love (Luke chapter 7 verse 47).

When the women reported the empty tomb to the disciples, most thought the women were talking nonsense, but Peter, in all fervour, ran straight to the tomb to see what had happened (Luke chapter 24 verse 12). Nothing was going to stop him from finding his Lord and Saviour again.

Forgiveness heals

We then read in John chapter 21, Jesus asks Peter three times – as many times as Peter had denied him, *"Simon son of John, do you love me?"*

Three times Peter replies, *"Yes lord, you know that I love you."*

Jesus gives him three commands, *"Feed my lambs"; "Take care of my sheep"; "Feed my sheep".*

And here we see Jesus' earlier prayer for Peter revisited:

> And when you have turned back, strengthen your brothers.
> (Luke chapter 22 verse 32)

Peter was about to enter a new era of ministry; the greatest ministry of his life was about to begin. This next leg began with failure, but this failure aligned him with the posture of humility he needed to have before God for God to be truly glorified in his life.

Jesus knew Peter would overcome and that he hadn't given him more than he could handle. He knew that Peter's faith was strong from the beginning and the truth was rooted deep within his heart. Even though Peter failed, God's words over him remained, and his failure was brought round in mighty strength to work for good, and cement a faith stronger than he had ever had in order for him to complete the good works that God had begun in him.

> Jesus replied, "Blessed are you, Simon son of Jonah, for this was not revealed to you by flesh and blood, but by my Father in heaven. And I tell you that you are Peter, and on this rock I will build my church, and the gates of Hades will not overcome it. I will give you the keys of the kingdom of heaven; whatever you bind on earth will be bound in heaven, and whatever you loose on earth will be loosed in heaven."
>
> (Matthew chapter 16 verses 17-20)

For Peter, there was purpose in his pain, and all things worked for his good because he loved the Lord. To this day, we are blessed and encouraged by his story, and by overcoming and holding onto God's promises in trials, people can be blessed by our stories too.

> I am coming soon. Hold onto what you have, so that no one will take your crown.
>
> (Revelation chapter 3 verse 11)

Chapter 22

HE WILL LIFT YOU UP IN DUE TIME

As I found the progression of my Bible readings reaching the short, four-chapter book called Ruth, I admit I didn't think I was going to get much out of it. I had read it a dozen or so times previously and, being happily married, I wasn't on the lookout for the 'perfect Boaz', as is so often the interpretation from this book. However, I was up to that book in my readings and, knowing it was short, I thought I'd skim through it. How wrong I was!

I got stuck on chapter two. It didn't speak to me of matchmaking, it spoke to me of the rewards of a hard-working woman, and it was like water to my soul.

A good work ethic

If you're anything like me, you're determined to work hard and work well at what God has put on your heart to do while still balancing all the balls in the air of family, friends and household management.

Well, with God's help and wisdom, we can do all that He has entrusted us with, and at just the right time, He will develop what He began in us for the purposes of His plan. If you haven't read the book of Ruth, I suggest you do.

Here are some great promises and wisdom from Ruth chapter two:

1. God has seen your hard work, and it has been (or will be) noticed by those that matter.

> ...she came into the field and has remained here from morning till now, except for a short rest in the shelter.
> (Ruth chapter 2 verse 6)

2. Don't be deterred from the work that God has given you to do. Keep doing what you're doing and stay within the safety of His 'field'.

> So Boaz said to Ruth, "My daughter, listen to me. Don't go and glean in another field and don't go away from here. Stay here with the women that work for me."
>
> (Ruth chapter 2 verse 8)

3. God will protect you so that your work is valued and rewarded. God is our defender and protector.

> Watch the field where the men are harvesting, and follow along after the women. I have told the men not to lay a hand on you.
>
> (Ruth chapter 2 verse 9)

4. Look after yourself, don't get worn out, refresh often.

> And whenever you are thirsty, go and get a drink from the water jars the men have filled.
>
> (Ruth chapter 2 verse 9)

5. Maintain a posture of humility.

> Why have I found such favour in your eyes that you notice me – a foreigner?
>
> (Ruth chapter 2 verse 10)

6. Whether you are a business owner or an employee, treat people well:

> You have put me at ease by speaking kindly to your servant – though I do not have the standing of one of your servants.
>
> (Ruth chapter 2 verse 13)

7. God will elevate you in His time. Boaz invited Ruth to his table.

> Come over here. Have some bread and dip it in the wine vinegar.
>
> (Ruth chapter 2 verse 14)

8. God's plan is over and above what we can imagine:

> When she sat down with the harvesters, he offered her some roasted grain. She ate all she wanted and had some left over.
>
> (Ruth chapter 2 verse 14)

9. Trust God to watch over you, to provide and protect.

> Boaz gave orders to his men, "Let her gather among the sheaves and don't reprimand her. Even pull out some stalks for her from the

bundles and leave them for her to pick up, and don't rebuke her."

(Ruth chapter 2 verse 15-16)

10. God will reward in His time. Though Naomi (Ruth's mother-in-law) had been through a time of famine in the past, at this point in time, they had returned as widows to a land of harvest and Ruth's hard work paid off. She brought home more than she could eat; she brought home enough to share with others through the kindness of Boaz's generosity.

> So Ruth gleaned in the field until evening. Then she threshed the barley she had gathered, and it amounted to about an ephah. She carried it back to town, and her mother-in-law saw how much she had gathered. Ruth also brought out and gave her what she had left over after she had eaten enough.
>
> (Ruth chapter 2 verses 17-18)

Blessings for the righteous

Boaz blessed the kindness and hard work of Ruth.

> May you be richly rewarded by the LORD, the God of Israel, under whose wings you have come to take refuge.
>
> (Ruth chapter 2 verse 12)

Naomi blessed the kindness of the man who noticed and generously provided for her and Ruth.

> May he be blessed by the LORD, whose kindness has not forsaken the living or the dead!
>
> (Ruth chapter 2 verse 20)

Kindness rewarded

Whether you are a business owner in charge of many employees, or an employer working for a business owner, when we honour the Lord with our hard work, honesty, kindness, fairness, and when we value others, we in turn will be blessed.

Ruth's hard work and efforts brought protection, generosity, provision, and blessing to others as well as herself. Boaz's kindness and fairness in his role as a leader over his workers brought him blessing and increased honour throughout the land.

When we adopt an attitude of valuing the gifts that God has given, when we don't give up but persevere through what we know is the path God has chosen for us and keep an attitude of humility, God will lift us up in His timing. He sees and knows and rewards.

Humble yourselves, therefore, under God's mighty hand, that he may lift you up in due time. Cast all your anxiety on him because he cares for you.

(1 Peter chapter 5 verses 6-8)

POEM

OH, LET ME DREAM!

Oh, let me dream of something new
In place where life has trodden,
The dreams I had, the wind, it blew
and now they seem forgotten.

But once again a freshness blows
and eagerly I wait,
to let it blow upon my face,
receiving at the gate.

A wholeness and a stirring noble,
awake my sleeping soul.
Restore the vigour of my youth,
upon which wings I'll soar.

For age it holds no grip on me,
my inner being states,
the longer that I've lived right here,
the greater land to take.

Rebecca Moore

Time's lessons only grow a strength
within me, that I know,
though bodies age and hairs grow grey,
my inner soul will glow.

The light within me draws its source
from One who is above
the solar systems, governments,
He is the One I love.

And as His love grows in my heart
the more I am amazed.
Oh, blow sweet breeze and fan the flame
and set my heart ablaze.

Therefore we do not lose heart. Though
outwardly we are wasting away, yet inwardly we
are being renewed day by day.
(2 Corinthians 4:16)

Chapter 23

ARE YOU REALLY LISTENING?

"Most of the successful people I've known are the ones who do more listening than talking."

—Bernard Baruch

A while ago, a good friend of mine asked me if I would like to do a podcast show with her. As we discussed what it would be about, we decided to put our focus on drawing out stories from everyday people. It has now been running for quite some time and we are amazed at what we have learned about people.

As we interview our guests and listen to stories of people who have overcome major obstacles in their lives, we are impressed at how they have each turned their negative experiences around to help others later in their lives. Some have had major accidents breaking multiple bones in their bodies, some have had abusive childhoods, some have overcome addictions, survived cancer, had loved ones die in awful circumstances, and one even became a missing person for a period of their life due to circumstances obviously not of their choosing.

It is surprising just what 40 minutes of deliberate and concentrated listening reveals!

Jesus the listener – listen to Jesus
The Bible talks a lot about listening. There are 23 references to listening in Proverbs alone. Recently I was reading the book of Luke, and the word 'listen' almost jumped off the page in multiple places.

When Jesus was a child, He spent time in the temple courts, 'sitting among the teachers, listening to them and asking them questions' (Luke chapter 2 verse 46). His understanding and answers amazed those who heard Him.

Then in Luke chapter 6 verse 27, Jesus makes a note of those who are listening:

> But to you who are listening I say: love your enemies, do good to those who hate you, bless those who curse you, pray for those who mistreat you…

He then distinguishes the difference between hearing and listening. He knows that many people hear words but are not really listening. Those who are really listening gain wisdom.

What's your foundation?

Sometimes we think we know better and don't need to listen. In Luke chapter 6 verses 46-49 Jesus describes what it's like for those who listen as compared to those who don't. And this is where we hear the parable of the wise and foolish builders; the foolish builders representing those who hear His words but don't put it into practice – who build on the ground without a foundation. The moment the torrent strikes, the house collapses. But for those who hear His words and put them into practice:

> They are like a man building a house, who dug down deep and laid the foundation on rock. When a flood came, the torrent struck that house but could not shake it, because it was well built.
>
> (Luke chapter 6 verse 48)

In Luke chapter 7 verse 1, Jesus distinguishes again that He is speaking with people who are listening.

> When Jesus had finished saying all this to the people who were listening, he entered Capernaum.

In Luke chapter 9, we hear straight from God a direction to listen to Jesus:

> A voice came from the cloud, saying, "This is my Son, whom I have chosen; listen to him."
> (v35)

It makes you stop to consider, doesn't it? Do we really listen? Or are we just hearing? I get the feeling that if we all really listened more intently to the words of Jesus, putting what He says into practice, and if we listened to the words and stories of others, there we would find some healing for those listened to, and wisdom for those who are listening, building a stronger firmer foundation for our 'house' to be built upon.

> Therefore consider carefully how you listen. Whoever has will be given more; whoever does not have, even what they think they have will be taken from them.
> (Luke chapter 8 verse 18)

Chapter 24

MAKE A JOYFUL NOISE

Have you ever heard someone complaining and it made you feel good? I can't say I have. Even if I agree with their complaints, I would rather it not be a problem to need to complain about in the first place.

Things happen that give us good reason to complain, of course, and injustice certainly needs attention, but it's not exactly something we'd want to make a habit of just for fun. Complaining makes me want to find a quick solution and look forward to the next conversation instead of the one I'm in.

Some of the emotions complaining draws out are heaviness, regret, sadness, and disappointment. Not exactly uplifting, is it? In fact, it is a draining experience that saps energy from both the complainer and the listener. And here I am complaining about complaining, ha! I apologise if you now feel deflated. Let's flip this!

When someone is joyous and excited about something, it has the opposite effect. It gives energy, inspires creativity and activity, it is soul-lifting and productive, giving way to more of what caused that joy to begin with. It makes you want to get on board with that person to increase and encourage the joy that moment has instigated.

Complaining gets you nowhere

The Israelites were good at complaining right up until the moment they were searching out the promised land they had travelled so long to receive. Even after God performed many miracles and led them out of the place where they had been slaves and fed them manna every day in the wilderness, the Israelites complained that maybe they would be better back in Egypt! They complained so much that God became angry, and Moses became so troubled he wanted to die.

> [Moses] They keep wailing to me, 'Give us meat to eat!' I cannot carry all these people by myself; the burden is too heavy for me. If this is how you are going to treat me, please

> go ahead and kill me – if I have found favour in your eyes – and do not let me face my own ruin.
>
> (Numbers chapter 11 verses 13-15)

Obviously complaining didn't draw good emotions from Moses, or God either!

> Now the people complained about their hardships in the hearing of the LORD, and when he heard them, his anger was aroused. Then fire from the LORD burned among them and consumed some of the outskirts of the camp.
>
> (Numbers chapter 11 verse 1)

When Moses sent leaders of the tribes to explore the promised land God was giving them, most came back fearful.

> The land we explored devours those living in it. All the people we saw there are of great size....We seemed like grasshoppers in our own eyes, and we looked the same to them.
>
> (Numbers chapter 13 verses 32-33)

Their complaining resulted in that generation missing out on entering the promised land – a high price to pay!

> … not one of those who saw my glory and the signs I performed in Egypt and in the wilderness but who disobeyed me and tested me ten times – not one of them will ever see the land I promised on oath to their ancestors. No one who has treated me with contempt will ever see it. But because my servant Caleb has a different spirit and follows me wholeheartedly, I will bring him into the land he went to, and his descendants will inherit it.
> (Numbers chapter 14 verses 22-24)

Personally, I find the alternative much more appealing.

Thankfulness
Caleb and Joshua returned with a glowing report. They had all seen the same things, yet Caleb and Joshua were hopeful, positive, and believing of the promise God had given them. They also trusted and knew that God would make a way for what He had promised.

Instead of complaining like the others, Caleb and Joshua made a joyful noise.

> The land we passed through is exceedingly good. If the LORD is pleased with us, he will lead us into that land, a land flowing with milk and honey, and will give it to us. Only do not rebel against the LORD. And do not be afraid of the people of the land, because we will devour them. Their protection is gone, but the LORD is with us. Do not be afraid of them.
>
> (Numbers chapter 14 verses 7-9)

Because of Caleb and Joshua's faith and trust in God to deliver them, God's heart was moved towards them, working for them, increasing their joy, and moving them into the space they were promised, declared, and believed for.

Just as we feel so much more willing to assist and make things happen when our children approach us with gratitude and joy, so too should be our attitude when we approach our Father in Heaven. When we make a joyful noise before the Lord, He receives us joyfully, increasing and encouraging the joy within us.

God's promised land for you is up ahead, or perhaps you are stepping into it. We can't approach it with fear and doubt, or we may miss out. Let's get our joy on, and however long it takes for that journey to come to pass, let's keep our eyes on the Lord, knowing that He is God, and we are His creation. How good are the things He has stored up for us!

> Make a joyful noise to the LORD, all the earth!
> Serve the LORD with gladness!
> Come into his presence with singing!
> (Psalm chapter 100 verses 1-2)

Chapter 25

WHAT MAKES GOD PROUD OF US?

Entering a season of weddings, we were privileged to witness the engagement of our eldest daughter Cartia to her fiancé Shane. It was a beautiful moment on a bridge in a Japanese garden surrounded by sprawling cherry blossom trees and neatly manicured lawns. Being in an open space, they were applauded at their public display of affection by excited onlookers.

Public declaration

On the day of their beautiful wedding, the happy couple publicly declared their love for each other as they became "joined in holy matrimony for as long as they both shall live". This public declaration was celebrated with cheers by all who attended and by all who joined in their celebrations near and far, drawing a happy tear or two from their mothers.

Public declarations come in all shapes and sizes be they weddings, marches, holiday celebrations, or protests, each require the declarer to be steadfast enough in what they are standing for in that moment – that they are proud enough and fearless to tell the world.

It reminds me of a song from the 90s by Christian pop group The Newsboys titled *Not Ashamed*. I remember being at their concert years ago listening to the words being declared unapologetically with strength and enthusiasm while strobe lights flew around a jumping, pumping crowd all singing:

> I'm not ashamed to let you know,
> I want this light in me to show
> I'm not ashamed to speak the name
> Of Jesus Christ
>
> What are we sneaking around for?
> Who are we trying to please?
> Shrugging off sin, apologising
> Like we're spreading some kind of disease
> I'm saying, "No way, No way."
>
> This one says it's a lost cause
> Save your testimonies for church time
> The other ones state you'd better wait
> Until you do a little market research
> I'm saying, "No way, No way"

Are we still so bold?

At a concert like that, it is easy to sing I'm not ashamed with a large crowd, but when it comes to day-to-day life, are we still so bold? Or have we been nullified and squashed by the culture of today that tells us everything is good for us, and nothing is bad?

While the world struggles to find itself right-side-up again after all the upheaval of the past few years, Jesus wants us to shine our lights bright like a lighthouse for those who are trying to find land.

It is not a time for hiding your light under a bushel.

In Luke chapter 12 verse 8, Jesus says:

> I tell you, whoever publicly acknowledges me before others, the Son of Man will also acknowledge before the angels of God. But whoever disowns me before others will be disowned before the angels of God.

If we want to know what makes God proud of us, this is it! We can't fear man more than God. It may take sacrifice, and you won't always be popular, but I think I'd much prefer to have eternity than be in the cool group, wouldn't you?

So then, as Jesus says in Matthew chapter 5 verses 14-16:

> You are the light of the world. A town built on a hill cannot be hidden. Neither do people light a lamp and put it under a bowl. Instead they put it on its stand, and it gives light to everyone in the house. In the same way, let your light shine before others, that they may see your good deeds and glorify your Father in heaven.

Chapter 26

IS THIS A DRESS-REHEARSAL?

My youngest daughter was to perform in a local theatre production. They had spent months learning lines, songs, and dances; the stage-sets, props, and costumes were prepared. The final thing that was required before the big performance, was to attend a dress rehearsal to make sure the many parts that make a successful production would come together on the night.

They knew well in advance this day was coming; they had helpers and teachers who taught and guided them, and they were now looking forward to the big day with great expectation. When the performance was to finally happen, they would not be surprised by it, but would draw on everything they had learned in order to get the final production right.

Are we surprised or ready?

The days we currently live in almost seem to have caught everyone by surprise. Are these the last days? Or is it preparation for them? There is much in the Bible that tells us about those times yet there is also much we don't know.

> At that time Michael, the great prince who protects your people, will arise. There will be a time of distress such as has not happened from the beginning of nations until then. But at that time your people—everyone whose name is found written in the book—will be delivered.
>
> (Daniel chapter 12 verse 1)

> Brother will betray brother to death, and a father his child. Children will rebel against their parents and have them put to death. Everyone will hate you because of me, but the one who stands firm to the end will be saved.
>
> (Mark chapter 13 verse 12-13)

While many parts of the globe are experiencing times of distress, and though we do not yet know how close we are to the final curtain call, we can still be in a state of readiness for whatever may come.

Repentance

In the letters to the seven churches (Revelation chapters 2-3), Jesus gives these warnings for repentance before the end so we can do a stocktake on the state of our hearts:

- **Return to your first love**
  You have forsaken the love you had at first. Consider how far you have fallen! Repent and do the things you did at first.

  (Revelation chapter 2 verses 4-5)

- **Reject idol worship and immorality**
  There are some among you who hold to the teaching of Balaam, who taught Balak to entice the Israelites to sin so that they ate food sacrificed to idols and committed sexual immorality…Repent therefore.

  (Revelation chapter 2 verse 14)

- **Beware of false prophets and deception**
  You tolerate that woman Jezebel, who calls herself a prophet. By her teaching she misleads my servants into sexual immorality and the eating of food sacrificed to idols.

  (Revelation chapter 2 verse 20)

- **Wake up!**

    You have a reputation of being alive, but you are dead. Wake up! Strengthen what remains and is about to die, for I have found your deeds unfinished in the sight of my God. Remember therefore, what you have received and heard; hold it fast, and repent. But if you do not wake up, I will come like a thief, and you will not know at what time I will come to you.

    (Revelation chapter 3 verses 1-3)

- **Be strong**

    I know your deeds, that you are neither cold nor hot. I wish you were either one or the other! So, because you are lukewarm – neither hot nor cold – I am about to spit you out of my mouth….be earnest and repent.

    (Revelation chapter 3 verses 15-16, 19)

It might sound harsh, but there's no time like the present to get ourselves right with God regardless of what season we are in. Infact, it is through God's mercy and grace that we are given time and warning.

Repeatedly throughout these letters, Jesus says, 'Whoever has ears, let them hear what the Spirit says to the churches.' And He says this because He wants us to be ready.

Unity

Never before have we seen such oppression on a global scale. But while the world looks dark, God is doing something greater.

> You intended to harm me, but God intended it for good to accomplish what is now being done, the saving of many lives.
> (Genesis chapter 50 verse 20)

While the enemy tries its hardest to cause disunity and separation, God is turning the tables because the enemy has overplayed his hand and many people are now looking for something greater and finding God.

When oppression and persecution happens, that is when God's people become strongest, and the church grows. While we follow the words of Jesus to love one another as He has loved us, and use wisdom and discernment for the days in which we are living, God's people become unified shaking the plans of the enemy to the core.

The more the enemy strategizes to spread fear, the more God's people are waking up and saying 'No' to the fear. We are finding courage we did not know we had. We are cultivating love which is 'the greatest of these' to bond with our brothers and sisters and care for each other.

The shaking
A shaking is certainly taking place. Perhaps this is a dress rehearsal – to refine us; for us to learn how to do things differently, and to get us in the right shape for the final performance.

Daniel chapter 11 verse 35 explains,

> Some of the wise will stumble, so that they may be refined, purified and made spotless until the time of the end, for it will still come at the appointed time.

Yet, God has not left us alone to work it out – not at all! He has sent the Holy Spirit as our helper to instruct us on all things. Acts chapter 2 verses 17-21 tells us:

> In the last days, God says, I will pour out my Spirit on all people. Your sons and daughters will prophesy, your young men will see

visions, your old men will dream dreams. Even on my servants, both men and women, I will pour out my Spirit in those days, and they will prophesy. I will show wonders in the heavens above and signs on the earth below, blood and fire and billows of smoke. The sun will be turned to darkness and the moon to blood before the coming of the great and glorious day of the Lord. And everyone who calls on the name of the Lord will be saved.

God has also equipped us with gifts and talents to help each other:

> So Christ himself gave the apostles, the prophets, the evangelists, the pastors and teachers, to equip his people for works of service, so that the body of Christ may be built up until we all reach unity in the faith and in the knowledge of the Son of God and become mature, attaining to the whole measure of the fullness of Christ.
>
> Then we will no longer be infants, tossed back and forth by the waves, and blown here and there by every wind of teaching and by

> the cunning and craftiness of people in their deceitful scheming. Instead, speaking the truth in love, we will grow to become in every respect the mature body of him who is the head, that is, Christ. From him the whole body, joined and held together by every supporting ligament, grows and builds itself up in love, as each part does its work.'
>
> (Ephesians chapter 4 verses 11-16)

So, whether this is the dress-rehearsal or the final performance, it is time for us to become one in Christ, caring for each other, building each other up in love, and preparing our pure white garments as the Bride of Christ ready for our beloved Bridegroom's return.

POEM

I HEARD THAT YOU WERE COMING

"I heard that you were coming,"
Said the young boy to the babe,
As he nestled near the manger
Where the new-born baby laid.

The baby squirmed and gurgled
In the sweet way babies do,
But he also had a look on him
As if much more he knew.

The young boy wriggled closer,
To gain a better view,
And these little ones locked eyes and smiled.
His heart within him grew.

To the sound of angels singing
And the wise men gathered by,
To the song of Mary's humming
And the glow of stars on high.

But this moment just between them,
In amongst this holy time,
Meant the world to this young boy,
Who quietly began to cry:

"You are such a special baby,
This I know within my heart,
And this isn't how the world would think
A great king's life would start.

But it's better, and I know,
If in a palace you were born,
Then people just like me
Would never feel your presence warm.

And I know that God in heaven
Placed you in this humble state,
For my father tells me stories,
What the prophets used to say."

At this the young boy paused,
And looked towards the baby's mum,
And then to Joseph's loving watch
To guard this precious son.

Lowering to a whisper
With a waver in his speech,
These careful words then followed
With the baby in his reach:

"They say things won't be easy
For you living on this earth,
They say that some will love you
But by others you'll be hurt."

The baby looked him in the eye,
Compassion through and through,
He gave a gorgeous little smile,
The boy knew that he knew.

And feeling sudden comfort
And reassurance strong,
His face grew slightly brighter
And then he sang this song:

"But you will be the Saviour
And bring peace into the earth.
Though wars and trials tarry,
Those you love, will know their worth.

And blind eyes will be opened,
And the mute tongues, they will sing.
The deaf will hear the sound of heaven,
Praises flow to Him.

And you will heal those who are sick,
The weary you'll restore,
And to those who will encounter you,
You'll open heaven's doors.

The heart will feel much lighter
As your presence enters in,
Your Holy Spirit filling them
As banished is their sin.

For you can see the banquet
That before us you have laid,
When you welcome us through heaven's gates,
How glorious that day!

And so, I want to thank you
For coming to this earth,
And living in this mess with us
And to an earthly birth.

Thank you for the love you have,
To suffer greatly so,
For there is no such greater love
That humankind can know.

For the joy that's set before you
As you gather those alone,
Is worth each bit of suffering
To bring your children home."

For the joy set before him he endured the cross, scorning its shame, and sat down at the right hand of the throne of God.
(Hebrews 12:2)

Chapter 27

THE BEST DAY EVER!

During the years of my children being at school, there have been a few days or more when they have lacked the desire to go to school. Comments like, "Do we have to go to school today?" and "I think I might be sick and need to stay home" (when obviously they weren't) – the whole dragging the feet after returning to school after six weeks of Christmas holidays etc…you know how it goes.

On days like these, I would often find myself saying with excitement, "You *have* to go to school today!" When they'd curiously ask why, I'd respond with, "Because today might just be the best day ever!"

Not what they were expecting
Then one day, it happened. Tony and I drove the kids to school, and as we drove into the school carpark, we

paused to let them out only to announce, "So, you're not going to school today. Instead, we're all going to Movie World!"

Let's just say, they didn't quite believe us at first. Then, as we drove away from the school towards the highway, the realisation came upon them that we were for real and they were excited, a little in disbelief, but also impressed that we had pulled off this surprise so well. I've got to say – I was a little impressed myself!

I had arranged a bag with a change of clothes in the back of the car and we were set to go, meeting more family members at the theme park when we arrived. We literally had 'the best day ever!' and our teenagers would have missed out on it if either of them had persisted in convincing me to let them stay home that day.

It took me years from when I first had the thought to actually carrying it out, then one day I decided, if I don't do it now, they'll have grown up and left school for good and we would never have had the fun spontaneous day that it turned out to be.

Expect it

There is another day I am really looking forward to – a day we need to be prepared for and keep constantly on our minds. This day truly will be 'the best day ever' and it is growing closer by the moment – the day when Jesus returns for His people.

> At that time people will see the Son of Man coming in clouds with great power and glory. And he will send his angels and gather his elect from the four winds, from the ends of the earth to the ends of the heavens.
> (Mark chapter 13 verses 26-27)

There is so much in the Bible about the return of Christ. I will try to keep it short and to the point, but please do some extended reading for yourself if you haven't already.

Firstly, we don't know the day or hour of Christ's return, but we can read the signs of the times which seem to be pointing to the probability that we're getting very close to it and we need to be ready – we always need to be ready. It's something you just won't want to miss out on.

Jesus talks about taking note of the times in Matthew chapter 24 verses 32-33:

> Now learn this lesson from the fig tree: As soon as its twigs get tender and its leaves come out, you know that summer is near. Even so, when you see all these things, you know that it is near, right at the door.

Matthew chapter 24 verses 37-39 tells us that it will be as it was in the days of Noah. Despite the warning, people carried on knowing nothing of what was coming until the flood engulfed them. Just as God provided an ark for Noah and his family, He will provide an 'ark' at the end of time too.

Preparation

In regard to being ready, Jesus tells the parable about the Ten Virgins in Matthew chapter 25:

> Five of them were foolish and five were wise. The foolish ones took their lamps but did not take any oil with them. The wise ones, however, took oil in jars along with their lamps.
>
> (verses 2-4)

When the bridegroom arrived, those who were prepared and ready were welcomed into the banquet, but the door was shut for those who were not prepared (paraphrased from verses 6-10).

It's going to be a great day for those who are prepared and ready, but awful for those who are not. However, there is still time, and while there is time – however short it may be – there is opportunity to take up the great gift of God called redemption through Jesus Christ, our Saviour. He is our Saviour because He saves us, and as Joel chapter 2 verse 32 says, '…everyone who calls on the name of the LORD will be saved.'

> The Lord is not slow in keeping his promise, as some understand slowness. Instead he is patient with you, not wanting anyone to perish, but everyone to come to repentance.
> (2 Peter chapter 3 verse 9)

The Benefits

We are reminded in Psalm 103, of the benefits of being in God's family:

> Praise the LORD, my soul,
> And forget not all his benefits—
> who forgives all your sins

> and heals all your diseases,
> who redeems your life from the pit
> and crowns you with love and compassion,
> who satisfies your desires with good things
> so that your youth is renewed like the eagle's.
>
> (Psalm 103 verses 2-5)

To be loved by the Creator, the one who made us, and gave everything for us to make it back home to Him, is the most wonderful gift we could ever imagine. We're talking about eternity – an eternity filled with love. I think that's worth being grateful and prepared for.

> So then, dear friends, since you are looking forward to this, make every effort to be found spotless, blameless and at peace with him. Bear in mind that our Lord's patience means salvation.
>
> (2 Peter 3 verse 14-15)

Make sure you're ready, today might just be *the best day ever!*

> Therefore keep watch because you do not know when the owner of the house will come back—whether in the evening, or at midnight, or when the rooster crows, or at

dawn. If he comes suddenly, do not let him find you sleeping. What I say to you, I say to everyone: 'Watch!'

(Mark chapter 13 verses 35-36)

Chapter 28

THE SIGNET RING

Lately I've been signing a lot of permission forms. With school comes excursions, school photos, subject changes, extra-curricular activities, camps…all of which need the authority of a parent's permission.

I'm glad that, though my youngest children are in high school, they're still young enough that I get to sign things for them, yet this time is quickly coming to an end. I hope that, as the time comes for them to have to sign things for themselves, they will have learned what they need in order to be responsible, kind and considerate adults who make wise decisions.

At that point, they will have their own authority to do things, authority that comes with having lived their first eighteen years learning right from wrong, learning what's wise and what's not, and to know it in their hearts.

Tried and tested

I once heard a great example in a sermon. The example was of the rigorous testing that a mobile phone manufacturer puts their product through before putting their branding on it. Once the phone has been tested to withstand elements and other trials, if it has endured and still works, then the manufacturer will seal it with their brand name. It is ready to represent the company.

Haggai chapter two tells of the trials the Jewish people had gone through to rebuild after their return from exile. When they turned their hearts to rebuild the house of God, He encouraged them to be strong and warned that He was going to shake the heavens and the earth. The Jews had been through so much testing, some had seen the house of God in its former glory before they had been sent into exile and now it looked like nothing.

There was, however, a greater glory coming, and God had marked His promise by anointing Zerubbabel as God's signet ring – His earthly representation.

> "On that day," declares the LORD Almighty, "I will take you, my servant Zerubbabel son of Shealtiel," declares the LORD, "and I will make you like my signet ring, for I have chosen you," declares the LORD Almighty.
>
> (Haggai chapter 2 verse 23)

Through Zerubbabel's line would come Jesus, the Saviour of the world, and the peace and freedom He would bring would be unlike anything that had ever existed before Him – freedom from sin, healing, daily help, joy, peace, and eternal life to all who believe.

God's Representatives

When we align our hearts with God's heart and allow God to work His purpose through our lives and become people who represent Him well, then we become like His signet ring. In Matthew chapter 16 verse 19, Jesus says to Peter:

> I will give you the keys of the kingdom of heaven; whatever you bind on earth will be bound in heaven, and whatever you loose on earth will be loosed in heaven.

To bind something, means to restrain it and secure it as with a rope. To loose something means to release or set something free which has been bound. With the keys of the kingdom of heaven, through Jesus' power we can tie up that which steals and destroys, and release that which restores and gives life – life in all its fulness.

It is not enough to float through life and just take things as they come when we have been given the keys to the kingdom to be vessels for God's will to be done on earth as it is in heaven. We need to wake from our slumber and make a difference to the lives of those around us through prayer, faith, and action.

To know God and to do His will on earth as it is in heaven, we need to study His Word, listen for His voice, know His ways, and obey His calling. The effects will begin like a little stream and grow into a flowing river as we trust Him and allow His power to work in and through our lives. When we work with God, we can 'sign on His behalf' through the power of the Holy Spirit and be world changers for the benefit of us all.

And if you ever forget the power that is at work within us, remember this:

> You, dear children, are from God and have overcome them, because the one who is in you is greater than the one who is in the world.
>
> (1 John chapter 4 verse 4)

Chapter 29

WEDDINGS!

Weddings! You've got to love them. They are special times in our lives full of love and expectation.

When our son Jesse was planning to pop the 'big question' to his beautiful girlfriend Bree, it was an exciting lead up. We knew what the plan was and what our roles in it were but were unable to give any secrets away – despite the multiple times Bree visited with our family. Life went on as normal as far as she was concerned, but for us, we knew the day was fast approaching.

The engagement

As it turned out, the plan worked, and Bree was completely surprised. The tickets to the performance in Brisbane we had bought for their birthdays served as a way to get Bree all dressed up and to the city with no clue as to what was coming. Following the concert, the couple strolled through the beautiful, landscaped gardens of Southbank with the lights of the buildings reflecting off the river, until they arrived at the perfect spot where Jesse asked the perfect question.

The photographer 'just happened' to be nearby and appeared in perfect timing, post the popping of the question, to take photos.

While this was happening, we had been able to organise to meet for dinner at Southbank with Bree's parents who were staying in Brisbane for a conference that very weekend. We 'just happened' to still be at the restaurant as Jesse and Bree 'just happened' to stroll towards us, faces beaming, to share the good news of an up-and-coming wedding. It was quite late by that time and one member of the family had to be woken up – Ben! (Every event needs a bit of humour).

Needless to say, we were all delighted! We were also relieved that the plan came off so well, with Bree none the wiser – just as it should be.

It was then time to plan the wedding!

The greatest wedding yet to come

Weddings are very important to Jesus. He often spoke in parables regarding weddings. All references to weddings pointed to the wedding of the Lamb as spoken of in Revelation chapter 19 verses 7-9:

> "Let us rejoice and be glad and give him glory! For the wedding of the Lamb has come, and his bride has made herself ready. Fine linen, bright and clean, was given her to wear." Then the angel said to me, "Write this: Blessed are those who are invited to the wedding supper of the Lamb!" And he added, "These are the true words of God."

The wedding supper of the Lamb is the uniting of God's people with Jesus their Saviour. It will be the ultimate celebration in the most beautiful of places. We don't know exactly when it will be, but we need to be alert and make ourselves ready, so we don't miss out.

The bridesmaids

Jesus' parable of a wedding in Matthew chapter 25 explains about 10 bridesmaids who were waiting for the groom to arrive. Some were ready, some were not. The bridegroom was taking a long time in coming and they fell asleep while waiting.

> At midnight the cry rang out: "Here's the bridegroom! Come out to meet him!"
>
> Then all the virgins woke up and trimmed their lamps. The foolish ones said to the wise, "Give us some of your oil; our lamps are going out."
>
> "No," they replied, "there may not be enough for both us and you. Instead, go to those who sell oil and buy some for yourselves."
>
> But while they were on their way to buy the oil, the bridegroom arrived. The virgins who were ready went in with him to the wedding. And the door was shut. Later the others also came. "Lord, Lord," they said, "open the door for us!" But he replied, "Truly I tell you, I don't know you."
>
> Therefore keep watch, because you do not know the day or the hour.

So how do we know when to be ready? Matthew chapter 24 verses 32-33 tells us:

> Now learn this lesson from the fig tree: As soon as its twigs get tender and its leaves come out, you know that summer is near. Even so, when you see all these things, you know that it is near, right at the door.

Just as Bree knew that one day Jesse would ask her to be his wife, she was unaware of when the exact time would be. But she knew the time was growing close and her heart was ready and prepared to give the answer.

The ark
God has prepared an 'ark' for us, and we are to help as many people to be heart-ready as possible, for sadly there will be a falling away which I think we are already seeing.

> At that time many will turn away from the faith and will betray and hate each other, and many false prophets will appear and deceive many people. Because of the increase of wickedness, the love of most will grow cold, but the one who stands firm to the end will be saved. And this gospel of the kingdom will be preached in the whole world as a testimony to all nations, and then the end will come.
> (Matthew 24 verses 10-14)

Some will let go of the hope that is coming, and even scorn it.

> Above all, you must understand that in the last days scoffers will come, scoffing and following their own evil desires. They will say, "Where is this 'coming' he promised? Ever since our ancestors died everything goes on as it has since the beginning of creation."
>
> (1 Peter chapter 3 verse 4)

Matthew chapter 24 verses 36-41 tells us that many people won't see it coming.

> But about that day or hour no one knows, not even the angels in heaven nor the Son, but only the Father. As in the days of Noah, so it will be at the coming of the Son of Man. For in the days before the flood, people were eating and drinking, marrying and giving in marriage, up to the day Noah entered the ark; and they knew nothing about what would happen until the flood came and took them all away. That is how it will be at the coming of the Son of Man. Two men will be in the field; one will be taken and the other left. Two women will be grinding with a hand mill; one will be taken and the other left.

The wedding

So, what will that day look like? 1 Thessalonians chapter 4 verses 15-18 says:

> For the Lord Himself will descend from heaven with a shout, with the voice of an archangel, and with the trumpet of God. And the dead in Christ will rise first. Then we who are alive and remain shall be caught up together with them in the clouds to meet the Lord in the air. And thus we shall always be with the Lord. Therefore comfort one another with these words.

And again in 1 Corinthians chapter 15 verses 51-52 tells us:

> Behold, I tell you a mystery: We shall not all sleep, but we shall all be changed—in a moment, in the twinkling of an eye, at the last trumpet. For the trumpet will sound, and the dead will be raised incorruptible, and we shall be changed.

And in Luke chapter 17 verse 24:

> For as the lighting that flashes out of one part under heaven shines to the other part under heaven, so also the son of Man will be in His day.

With warnings we can be prepared, but what a disaster if we are not! This will not be a wedding to be locked out of.

> For then there will be great distress, unequalled from the beginning of the world until now—and never to be equalled again.
> (Matthew chapter 24 verse 21)

So now, as the groom looks forward to making his bride his wife, we prepare for the wedding, we keep watch, we gather what needs to be gathered, and give what needs to be given.

> And this gospel of the kingdom will be preached in the whole world as a testimony to all nations.
> (Matthew chapter 24 verse 14)

It is not a time for sleeping but a time to celebrate, to send invitations, and prepare for a great feast!

Chapter 26

THOUGH IT HAS ENDED, YET, IT HAS JUST BEGUN…

Walking through the final days of the year, I felt somewhat grateful. I didn't revel in the gladness of seeing a bad year come to an end (though there have been years like that). For me, it had been a satisfying year in accomplishing what I'd set out to complete from the previous year's resolutions and I felt quite happy with it. Perhaps it was a good time to take a year off…think again!

My next yearly planner was already healthily filling out like a well-planned menu, and I was determined to hit the ground running to see these things come to pass. However, I knew these plans would require a lot of hard work and action but, no matter how much I'd prepare, at the end of the coming year, I knew I would see God's unmistakable guidance and weaving stamped all over it, which, gratefully, would make my current pencilled-in plans look very amateur in the grander scheme of things.

> Many are the plans in a person's heart, but it is the LORD'S purpose that prevails.
> (Proverbs chapter 19 verse 21)

Power in the present
Despite how successful or unsuccessful our pasts have been, whether relational, financial, or whatever they may be – the past will always be our past and has no power for the present unless we allow it. The stories and experiences we take with us can either propel us, positively influence us and give us wisdom for the future; or they will hold us down, hold us back and cause us to be stuck in a place we can't get out of. It is up to us what we choose to take with us on the journey ahead. Wisdom comes in knowing which parts of our past are freeing and empowering, and which are those that take us captive.

We may automatically refer to negative experiences as being what we should leave behind, and rightly so in many circumstances. Though often, some negative past experiences can give us the drive and motivation we need to make improvements for the future.

Surprisingly, however, sometimes our past triumphs and successes can also hold us back from moving forward.

Now is not the time to sleep

Our experiences have the power to either hold us back in a state of 'reminiscence', or project us into the future to bigger and better things. Our experiences ultimately determine the outcome of our character; who we become if we choose to focus our attention on the future. What we can accomplish in the future and how we can better ourselves for the future is up to the way we process the past and allow God to use it for our good.

> "For I know the plans I have for you," declares the LORD, "plans to prosper you and not to harm you, plans to give you hope and a future."
>
> (Jeremiah chapter 29 verse 11)

God doesn't want us to fall asleep. The work at hand is now. Future thinking, or forward thinking, is what we need to be focusing on. Not the lives we lived yesterday, but the days we will live in the future and how we develop ourselves and our character in order to be better and brighter people.

As we step into new spaces, is our perspective one of embracing new opportunities that lay before us? Or are we so entrenched in our past successes and failures that we dare not move on?

Jesus wants more for us
When Jesus was on the earth, He did amazing things. He healed, revealed truth, and brought salvation to a dying world, fulfilling many prophecies and opening the way for future generations. He did so many things that the Bible tells us: if each were written down, there would not be enough room in the world for all the books that would be written! (John chapter 21 verse 25)

But when He died on the cross, it was not the end; it was the beginning. He told the disciples, in John chapter 14 verse 12, that they would go on to do even greater things, through the power of the Holy Spirit! When Jesus healed people, He wanted them to use their healed, working, able bodies to do things – things to help others – otherwise the healing would be a waste. Even if our bodies aren't fully working, as long as we have breath, we have mighty purpose.

When God gives us a new day, He wants us to use our time on earth to carry His presence, to be a blessing, and to bring people closer to Him through the gifts He has given us, and He has promised to be with us and help us every step of the way.

> Therefore go and make disciples of all nations, baptizing them in the name of the Father and of the Son and of the Holy Spirit, and teaching them to obey everything I have commanded you. And surely I am with you always, to the very end of the age.
> (Matthew chapter 28 verses 19-20)

God likes to put His stamp on our life
As we reflect on and gather the memories of the collection of experiences that we have had in our lives, let's put them to good use. Let's make a resolution to use the good and bad for a brighter future. Let's use our bodies and minds to do great things, to be useful and to be a blessing to others by enlarging our tents, expanding our reach, growing in strength, and carrying the Word of God to the ends of the earth.

God has great things in store for us and in His strength, with willing hearts, we can be His vessel to accomplish much in His name.

Enlarge the place of your tent, stretch your tent curtains wide, do not hold back; lengthen your cords, strengthen your stakes. For you will spread out to the right and to the left; your descendants will dispossess nations and settle in their desolate cities. Do not be afraid; you will not be put to shame. Do not fear disgrace; you will not be humiliated. You will forget the shame of your youth and remember no more the reproach of your widowhood. For your Maker is your husband—the LORD Almighty is his name—the Holy One of Israel is your Redeemer; he is called the God of all the earth.

(Isaiah chapter 54 verses 2-5)

POEM

THIS NEW DAY

Where once the brandied river flowed
Towards the ocean's seam,
The flower and the paddock snowed
Green bounty now unseen.

Washed white with moonlit colours bright,
The flashing of the glow,
The flowered beds are now at rest,
Old memories live below.

But as the chilling melts away,
Though soggy mud appears,
The fine green spears of fresh new growth
Bring music to my ears.

The lambs begin to murmur
Their bleating, oh so sweet!
And one by one dear little ones
Find strength upon their feet.

Rebecca Moore

Buds open as they see the sky
And happy birds go flying by,
A scent of freshness in the air
And children play without a care.

And so, the river flows again,
Washing old away,
And carries with it, happiness
That speaks of this new day.

See, I am doing a new thing! Now it springs up; do you not perceive it? I am making a way in the wilderness and streams in the wasteland.
(Isaiah 43:19)

ALSO BY REBECCA MOORE
First To Forty

First to Forty is a collection of Rebecca's first forty short inspirational articles and poems about womanhood and everyday life.

Laugh, giggle and cry as Rebecca shares life's journey in a way that makes your life a home, and those you love its most valued treasures.

A must-read for every mother.

ISBN: 978-0-6484602-1-3

Pizza & Choir

With a masterful touch, loving heart, and joyful perspective in life, Rebecca captures and retells the moments in our lives that really matter.

This collection of short stories, poems and prose will brighten your every day and have you smiling, laughing out loud, crying and making the most of life's precious moments.

Pizza & Choir is a beautiful view of life.

ISBN: 978-0-6484602-0-6